Better Homes and Gardens®

Calorie-Trimmed Recipes

On the front cover: *Spicy Pork Skillet, Elegant Chicken Crepes,* and *Sweet and Sour Pork Skillet.* **On the back cover:** *Beefy Tossed Salad* and *Ham and Cottage Cheese Molds.* (See index for recipe pages.)

BETTER HOMES AND GARDENS® BOOKS

Editor: Gerald M. Knox
Art Director: Ernest Shelton

Food and Nutrition Editor: Doris Eby
Senior Food Editor: Sharyl Heiken
Senior Associate Food Editors: Sandra Granseth, Elizabeth Woolever
Associate Food Editors: Bonnie Lasater, Marcia Stanley, Joy Taylor, Pat Teberg, Diana Tryon
Recipe Development Editor: Marion Viall
Test Kitchen Director: Sharon Golbert
Test Kitchen Home Economists: Jean Brekke, Kay Cargill, Marilyn Cornelius, Maryellyn Krantz, Marge Steenson

Associate Art Directors: Neoma Alt West, Randall Yontz
Copy and Production Editors: David Kirchner, Lamont Olson, David A. Walsh
Assistant Art Director: Harijs Priekulis
Senior Graphic Designer: Faith Berven
Graphic Designers: Linda Ford, Sheryl Veenschoten, Tom Wegner

Editor-in-Chief: James A. Autry
Editorial Director: Neil Kuehnl
Group Administrative Editor: Duane Gregg
Executive Art Director: William J. Yates

Calorie-Trimmed Recipes
Editor: Joy Taylor
Copy and Production Editor: David A. Walsh
Graphic Designer: Sheryl Veenschoten

Contents

Weight Control

You are not alone if you're "watching what you eat." Many people today are trying to either lose a few pounds or maintain their waistline. Whichever is your goal, calories are a main concern in any weight control program, and that's where this book helps. Throughout it – and especially on the next few pages – you'll find basic information about planning and preparing calorie-trimmed meals that are satisfying and nutritious. You'll discover that you can prepare delicious, low-calorie recipes using everyday foods, that you don't need dietary products or special "health foods."

The means for calorie trimming and weight control are all here. You need supply only one essential ingredient: will power!

Calories

Calories, calories, calories! You hear and talk about them and sometimes even worry about them. But what exactly are they?

Calories are units of measure of the energy supplied by specific foods. You need a certain number of calories daily just to sustain life. And you obtain them through foods, with each food varying in the amount of calories it supplies. Protein, carbohydrate, and fat are the nutrient sources of calories. Proteins and carbohydrates provide four calories per gram; fats have nine calories per gram. Alcohol provides seven calories per gram, but has little nutritional value.

It is important to evaluate foods for their nutrient makeup as well as their calorie count. Foods may have approximately the same amount of calories but vary greatly in their nutritional contribution to a diet. For example, an apple has 80 calories and adds vitamins to the diet; one cup of a carbonated cola beverage has 96 calories, yet it contributes next to nothing nutritionally.

Body weight is maintained when calorie intake equals calories used for energy. When the intake of calories exceeds your body's energy expenditure, you gain weight (usually in the form of stored fat). Each pound of excess body fat represents 3,500 calories of unused energy. Thus, you can easily calculate your calorie needs. To lose one pound a week, you must reduce your food intake by 3,500 calories per week; to lose two pounds: 7,000 calories.

You need to know how many calories your body needs to maintain your ideal weight. For an estimate of daily energy needs, the United States Department of Agriculture suggests you allow yourself 14 to 26 calories per pound of desirable weight, depending on your sex, age, and amount of physical activity. You can figure the approximate number of daily calories you need to maintain your ideal weight by multiplying your ideal weight by one of the numbers in the column at right. In order for these calculations to be helpful, be realistic when considering your activity level! (See page 6 for levels of activity.)

Activity	Females per pound	Males per pound
Sedentary	14 calories	16 calories
Moderately active	18 calories	21 calories
Very active	22 calories	26 calories

For example, a woman weighing 128 pounds, aged 23 to 50, whose level of activity is sedentary, uses approximately 14 calories per pound per day to maintain body weight — a total of 1,792 calories. A 154-pound man in the same age and activity range uses 16 calories per pound a day or 2,464 calories.

To lose weight at the medically recommended rate of one to two pounds per week you have to give up 500 to 1,000 calories a day or burn that many calories through exercise. Hence, the 128-pound woman, who wants to lose 5 pounds in 5 weeks, should limit herself to 1,292 calories per day. (To lose more than one pound per week she should increase her exercise level.)

Cutting back on your caloric intake may look easy on paper, but it is no easy task actually. Here are some helpful suggestions.

Stretching Calories

You can make calorie-trimming easier throughout a day in several ways.
Eat more slowly. It's easier to tell when you've had enough to eat if you don't gobble up your meals.
Cut down on the size of the portions. If you want to feel less deprived, use a smaller plate than usual.
Stretch your meals. Try setting aside a part of your normal meal, so that you have four or five mini-meals a day. Frequent meals help reduce your eating "extra" foods.
Select filling, low-calorie snacks. Keep nutritious nibbles handy for easy munching; try fresh fruits and vegetables, vegetable juice cocktail, diet soda, or consommé.
Release your tensions by expanding energy. If the refrigerator beckons when you're pent up, a brisk walk around the block can be a satisfying alternative to food.
Limit the areas where you eat. Eat all your meals and snacks in the kitchen or dining room; consider all other rooms out of bounds.
Concentrate on eating. If you eat while reading or watching television you can unconsciously overeat.
Eat formally. Whenever you eat, serve the food on a plate, even if you are having just a light snack. Sit yourself down at the kitchen or dining room table. A dislike for dishwashing may help curb your appetite.
Don't keep your goal a secret. The support of your family and friends can strengthen your resolve.
Make calorie counting and exercise a way of life. As people get older, they tend to become more sedentary, and the disparity between food intake and energy expended causes them to gain weight. The body's basic requirements for calories decreases with age, meaning a person will gain weight unless he consumes fewer calories.

Studies indicate that the healthiest persons are those who reach their adult weight level and remain stable thereafter. In other words, an adult's weight should be the same at age 50 as it was at 25.

Unfortunately for most of us, that means gradually cutting down on what we eat as we get older. Hard, yes; but the rewards are well worth the sacrifice.

Nutritional Analysis

Every recipe in this book has a nutritional analysis. This analysis gives values for the amount of calories, proteins, carbohydrates, fats, sodium, and potassium in an individual serving of the recipe. The analysis also gives the percentages of the United States Recommended Daily Allowances (U.S. RDA) (see page 9) for protein, vitamin A, vitamin C, thiamine, riboflavin, niacin, and iron per serving. Use the nutritional analyses to compare the nutritional values of recipes. Plan your daily menus (see pages 8 and 9) by finding recipes that meet your calorie and nutritional needs. For ease of comparison of recipes within a chapter, we have put the nutritional analyses in chart form in the beginning of each chapter.

The information for nutritional analysis comes from a computerized method using Agriculture Handbook No. 456 by the United States Department of Agriculture. The values found for the recipes in *Calorie-Trimmed Recipes* are as correct and complete as possible.

To obtain the nutritional analyses we made some assumptions:
—Suggested garnishes were omitted in the analyses.
—If a food was marinated and then brushed with the marinade during cooking, the analysis includes the nutritional information of the entire amount of marinade.
—For main dish meat recipes, the nutritional analyses were calculated using measurements for cooked lean meat, trimmed of fat.
—When two ingredient options appear in a recipe, the nutritional analysis was calculated using the first choice of ingredients.
—When a recipe ingredient has a variable weight (such as a 2½- to 3-pound broiler-fryer chicken) the nutritional analysis was calculated using the lesser weight of the ingredient.

Exercise & Weight Table

Calorie intake and output are not all that mystifying. Put simply: That which goes in must be used up or you'll gain weight. Extra calories eaten above the daily requirement are stored as fat. The only way to lose this fat is to eat less (consume fewer calories), exercise more (burn off excess calories), or combine the two. Studies indicate that a combination of reducing calories and increasing exercise has tremendous beneficial effects on the body: Body fat is reduced and physical fitness is achieved. Physical fitness improves cardiovascular endurance, flexibility, muscular strength, muscular endurance, and body composition. The overall effect is improved appearance and self-esteem, a feeling of vitality and healthiness, and enhanced physical abilities.

Starting an exercise program requires effort and concentration. Evaluate your eating and exercise habits, and make any necessary changes. Gear your exercise to match your physical condition, schedule, and space where you can easily exercise. Set some goals, such as "walk to the grocery store" or "swim twice a week." Make your goals simple and add more activities as you go along, but be persistent. Regular moderate exercise benefits you more than occasional strenuous exercise. Seek exercises and activities you enjoy: Things you like probably will become habit-forming. Let exercise become an important part of your life. If you fail occasionally, don't become discouraged; the times you exercise will make up for any occasional lapses.

BURNING CALORIES

Below are *estimates* of the *total* calories burned per hour doing several types of activities. Of course, calories used during exercise vary with the intensity of the performance. You can perform the same exercise yet burn off more calories if you step up the pace. And some individuals perform certain exercises more efficiently than others do, thus burning fewer calories. Calorie expenditure also is affected by an individual's sex, age, and size.

Sedentary Activities–80 to 100 calories expended per hour			
lying down	typing	sewing	
sitting	sleeping	light office work	

Light Activities–110 to 160 calories expended per hour			
cooking	standing	washing dishes	
ironing	driving	walking slowly	

Moderate Activities–170 to 240 calories expended per hour			
dressing	making beds	walking moderately fast	
laundry	carpentry work	light gardening	

Vigorous Activities–250 to 350 calories expended per hour			
golf	gardening	heavy housework	
bowling	walking briskly	bicycling moderately fast	

Strenuous Activities–360 calories or more expended per hour			
jogging	tennis	skiing	football
dancing	swimming	skating	soccer

HEIGHT/WEIGHT TABLE

The table below gives estimates of the ideal weight for adults to maintain throughout life. Remember: Each person is an individual and normal weight in healthy adults varies over a wide range.

Persons with a larger than average build (wide shoulders and hips, large wrists and ankles) should weigh between the average and high figures given in the table. Persons with small builds (narrow shoulders and hips, small wrists and ankles) probably should weigh no more than the average and no less than the low figure given for their height. Don't use the height/weight table to justify any extra weight by claiming that your body frame is bigger than it actually is.

WOMEN height (feet and inches)	low	average	high
5'	100 pounds	109 pounds	118 pounds
5'1"	104 pounds	112 pounds	121 pounds
5'2"	107 pounds	115 pounds	125 pounds
5'3"	110 pounds	118 pounds	128 pounds
5'4"	113 pounds	122 pounds	132 pounds
5'5"	116 pounds	125 pounds	135 pounds
5'6"	120 pounds	129 pounds	139 pounds
5'7"	123 pounds	132 pounds	142 pounds
5'8"	126 pounds	136 pounds	146 pounds
5'9"	130 pounds	140 pounds	151 pounds
5'10"	133 pounds	144 pounds	156 pounds
5'11"	137 pounds	148 pounds	161 pounds
6'	141 pounds	152 pounds	166 pounds
MEN			
5'3"	118 pounds	129 pounds	141 pounds
5'4"	122 pounds	133 pounds	145 pounds
5'5"	126 pounds	137 pounds	149 pounds
5'6"	130 pounds	142 pounds	155 pounds
5'7"	134 pounds	147 pounds	161 pounds
5'8"	139 pounds	151 pounds	166 pounds
5'9"	143 pounds	155 pounds	170 pounds
5'10"	147 pounds	159 pounds	174 pounds
5'11"	150 pounds	163 pounds	178 pounds
6'	154 pounds	167 pounds	183 pounds
6'1"	158 pounds	171 pounds	188 pounds
6'2"	162 pounds	175 pounds	192 pounds
6'3"	165 pounds	178 pounds	195 pounds

The measurements in this chart are without shoes or clothing.

Nutrition

Foods supply essential nutrients to our bodies and our nutritional requirements are basically constant whether we're on high- or low-calorie diets. To approach your diet sensibly, you really should know some nutritional basics.

Food is composed of proteins, carbohydrates, fats, vitamins, minerals, and water — altogether more than 50 essential nutrients. Most foods contain several nutrients, but no one food contains them all. If you have normal nutritional requirements, a diet high in one nutrient (such as protein) and low in another (such as carbohydrate) will never meet your needs. To get all the nutrients you need and be satisfied, too, you must eat a variety of foods for a balanced diet. Here's why we need certain nutrients.

Nutrients

Protein (amino acids) is needed for the body's building, maintaining, and repairing jobs. It provides energy if there is inadequate carbohydrate or fat present. The body needs to be replenished with protein several times each day. Adult females need 44 grams protein a day and adult males need 56 grams.

Carbohydrates (sugars and starches) provide the energy for your body. If carbohydrate intake is too low, the body compensates by manufacturing energy from protein, which can result in a protein shortage. A common misconception is that carbohydrate-containing foods are fattening, but carbohydrates actually supply no more energy (that is, calories) than do proteins. Excessive carbohydrates that aren't needed for energy are stored as fat, but this is true of dietary fats and protein also.

Fats provide a highly concentrated form of energy — more than twice that of carbohydrates or proteins and are essential in any diet. Fat in our diet supplies an indispensable fatty acid necessary to life; it also carries vitamins A, D, E, and K throughout the body. Energy stored in the body in the form of fat provides a protective cushion around vital organs and protects the body from rapid temperature changes.

Vitamins are essential for chemical reactions throughout the body. Each known vitamin performs a specific function that no other nutrient can. Our bodies cannot manufacture most vitamins, so they need to be in the foods we eat. A deficiency of just one vitamin can have an effect on long-term fitness. Excessive doses of some vitamins also can cause adverse reactions within the body. *Vitamin A* is needed for bone growth, healthy tooth structure, development of normal skin, and it aids in night vision. Large amounts of this vitamin can be stored in the liver, but excess doses may be toxic. *Vitamin C* (ascorbic acid) is necessary for the framework of bones and teeth and for healthy gums and blood vessels. Vitamin C is unstable and easily destroyed so it needs to be consumed every day. *Vitamin E* prevents the oxidation and breakdown of cells and substances such as vitamins A and D. Deficiencies are rare. *Vitamin D* aids in proper utilization of calcium and phosphorus in bones. Vitamin D can be synthesized by the action of the sun's rays on the skin. Excess doses may have toxic effects. *Vitamin K* is needed for normal blood clotting. Deficiency is rare. *Thiamine* regulates appetite and digestion, maintains healthy nerves, and helps release energy from food. Thiamine is not stored in the body so it needs to be replenished in the diet every day. *Riboflavin* aids in the process of food metabolism, promotes healthy skin and mouth, helps cells use oxygen, and aids vision in bright light. Riboflavin is not stored in the body and needs to be replenished at frequent intervals. Deficiency is rare. *Niacin* is involved in the conversion of sugars to energy and fat synthesis. It keeps the skin, digestive tract, and nervous system healthy. Niacin needs to be in a food source daily.

Minerals regulate bodily processes, too, and need to be provided by foods in our daily diet. *Calcium* gives strength and structure to bones, and rigidity and permanence to teeth. About 99% of the body's calcium is contained in bones and teeth. The remaining 1% is important for blood clotting, muscle contraction, and nerve impulses. *Iron* is an important constituent of every red blood cell in the body. It carries oxygen throughout the body. Blood loss or lack of sufficient iron in the diet can cause iron-deficiency anemia. Toxic levels of iron are extremely rare. *Sodium* (salt) helps regulate the passage of water and nutrients out of cells and helps maintain the proper acid-base balance in body fluids. The average diet furnishes about three times as much sodium as is needed. The estimated safe and adequate daily intake of sodium is 1,100 to 3,300 milligrams for adults. *Potassium* also regulates acid-base balance in body fluids. It regulates muscular excitability and contraction, and aids in protein synthesis. A diet that is adequate in protein, calcium, and iron also contains adequate potassium. The estimated safe and adequate daily intake of potassium is 1,875 to 5,625 milligrams for adults.

These nutrients, plus more, need to be in the foods we eat. The amount of the nutrient and the combination of nutrients in our food is important. Eating a variety of foods ensures the body's needs are met. The *United States Recommended Daily Allowances (U.S. RDA)* and the *Basic Five Food Groups* serve as guides to meet nutritional needs.

Meeting Nutritional Needs

The *Recommended Dietary Allowances (RDA)* tell the amounts of certain nutrients necessary to meet the nutritional needs of practically all healthy people over time. RDAs have been set for 17 different population groups based on age, sex, weight, and certain physical conditions (such as pregnancy and lactation). The *United States Recommended Daily Allowances (U.S. RDA)* are simplified and condensed RDAs used on nutrition labeling. The nutritional analyses in this book give the percentage *U.S. RDA* of protein, vitamin A, vitamin C, thiamine, riboflavin, niacin, calcium, and iron.

When planning menus, choose a variety of foods so that over a period of time they meet the U.S. RDA for each nutrient. The nutritional analysis charts are useful for estimating an adequate intake of each nutrient. Another approach to ensure nutritional needs are met is to use the *Basic Five Food Groups* system. This flexible system takes into account the RDAs. By selecting the proper number of servings from the food groups every day, you can obtain the nutrients essential to good health.

Milk-Cheese Group: Foods in this group supply calcium, riboflavin, protein, vitamin A, and sometimes vitamin D (as in the case of vitamin D fortified milk.) Milk and milk products are the major source of calcium in the American diet. Children younger than 12 should drink 2 to 3 cups milk daily; children 12 and older, 3 to 4 cups; and adults, 2 cups. Dairy products equivalent to 1 cup milk include 1 cup plain yogurt, 2 ounces process cheese food, 2 cups cottage cheese, ¼ cup Parmesan cheese, 1½ ounces cheddar or Swiss cheese, and 1½ cups ice cream. Low-fat or skim milk products such as yogurt have the same nutrients as whole-milk products but fewer calories.

Meat-Poultry-Fish-Beans Group: These foods are the main sources of protein, phosphorus, and iron. You should eat two servings from this group every day. One serving is equal to: 2 to 3 ounces of cooked lean meat, poultry, or fish without bone; 2 eggs; ½ to 1 cup nuts, sesame seeds, or sunflower seeds; ¼ cup peanut butter. Cooked dry beans, dry peas, and lentils are also in this group but are higher in calories.

Vegetable-Fruit Group: Fruits and vegetables provide vitamin A and vitamin C. From this group, you should have four servings every day, including one good vitamin C source (citrus fruit or juice). Every other day include one good vitamin A source (dark-green or deep-yellow vegetables). One serving equals ½ cup or a portion ordinarily served, such as a wedge of lettuce or ½ grapefruit. Most fruits and vegetables are low in fat.

Bread-Cereal Group: One serving equals 1 slice whole grain or enriched bread, 1 ounce ready-to-eat cereal, ½ to ¾ cup cooked cereal, cornmeal, pasta, or rice. These foods supply thiamine, niacin, riboflavin, and iron. Four servings should be consumed every day.

Fats-Sweets-Alcohol Group: Foods in this group supply mainly calories with few nutrients. This would include butter, margarine, mayonnaise, salad dressings, candy, sugar, jelly, soft drinks, alcoholic beverages, and unenriched breads and pastries. No serving sizes are suggested. The amount of these foods in your diet depends on how many calories you need.

While counting calories, be especially careful when choosing foods from each food group. Look for low-calorie sources of important nutrients. Compare the calorie counts of foods in the same food group using the chart on pages 10 through 13. Try to keep away from the Fats-Sweets-Alcohol Group, which mainly contributes calories to the diet.

Calorie Counts

Make calorie counting a daily habit. Be aware that snacking on candy, nuts, and soft drinks can quickly add up to hundreds of calories. Check here when in doubt about the caloric value of a food. You may discover that the foods you thought were low-calorie are actually the culprits sabotaging your diet.

Plan daily menus to meet nutritional needs and use this chart to keep tabs on your calorie intake. To figure the calories per serving of a favorite family recipe, find the calorie count of each recipe ingredient. Add up all the calorie counts, then divide by the number of servings the recipe makes.

A-B

ANCHOVY, canned; 5 fillets 35
APPLE
   fresh; 1 medium 80
   juice, canned; 1 cup 117
APPLESAUCE, canned
   sweetened; ½ cup 116
   unsweetened; ½ cup................50
APRICOT
   canned, in syrup; ½ cup 111
   dried, cooked, unsweetened,
     in juice; ½ cup 106
   fresh; 3 medium 55
   nectar; 1 cup 143
ASPARAGUS
   cooked, drained; 4 spears 12
   fresh cut spears; 1 cup 35
AVOCADO, peeled, all varieties
   ½ avocado 188
BACON
   2 crisp strips,
     medium thickness..................86
   Canadian-style, cooked; 1 slice......58
BANANA; 1 medium 101
BARBECUE SAUCE, bottled; ½ cup .114
BEANS
   baked, with tomato sauce
     and pork, canned; ½ cup 155
   green snap, canned; ½ cup.............21
   green snap, fresh; ½ cup 17
   green snap, frozen; ½ cup 17
   lima, cooked; ½ cup 95
   red kidney, canned; ½ cup 115
   white, dry, cooked; ½ cup 112
   yellow or wax, cooked; ½ cup........14
BEAN SPROUTS, fresh; ½ cup........18
BEEF, dried, chipped; 2 ounces 116
BEEF CUTS
   corned, canned; 3 ounces 184
   ground beef, cooked
     10 percent fat; 3 ounces 186
     21 percent fat; 3 ounces 233
   pot roast, cooked
     lean and fat; 3 ounces................246
     lean only; 3 ounces 164

   rib roast, cooked
     lean and fat; 3 ounces..............375
     lean only; 3 ounces 205
   round steak, cooked;
     3 ounces 161
   sirloin steak, broiled;
     3 ounces 329
BEEF LIVER, fried; 2 ounces 130
BEETS, cooked, diced; ½ cup...........13
BEVERAGES, alcoholic
   beer; 1 cup 101
   dessert wine; 1 ounce..................41
   gin, rum, vodka – 80 proof;
     1 jigger 97
   table wine; 1 ounce 25
BISCUIT, enriched baking powder;
   1 (2-inch diameter)................103
BLACKBERRIES
   canned in syrup; ½ cup 116
   fresh; ½ cup 42
BLUEBERRIES
   fresh; ½ cup 45
   frozen, sweetened; ½ cup 121
BOUILLON
   instant granules; 1 teaspoon..............2
BOYSENBERRIES, frozen,
   unsweetened; ½ cup................30
BREAD
   Boston brown; 1 slice
     (3¼x½ inch) 95
   breadstick, plain; 1
     (7¾ inches long) 19
   corn; 1 piece
     (2½ inches square) 161
   crumbs, dry; ¼ cup 98
   crumbs, soft; ¾ cup 30
   cubes; 1 cup 81
   French; 1 slice
     (½ inch thick) 44
   Italian; 1 slice
     (½ inch thick) 28
   pumpernickel; 1 slice 79
   raisin; 1 slice 66
   rye; 1 slice 61
   Vienna; 1 slice
     (½ inch thick) 73
   white; 1 slice 68
   whole wheat; 1 slice 56

BROCCOLI
   cooked; 1 medium stalk 47
   frozen chopped, cooked; ½ cup 24
BRUSSELS SPROUTS, cooked;
   ½ cup....................................28
BUTTER: 1 tablespoon 102

C

CABBAGE
   Chinese, raw; ½ cup.........................6
   common varieties, raw,
     shredded; 1 cup 17
   red, raw, shredded; 1 cup 22
CAKE, baked from home recipes
   angel, no icing; 1/12 cake.................161
   chocolate, 2 layers,
     chocolate icing; 2-inch wedge ...365
   fruitcake; 1 slice
     (¼x2x1½ inches).........................57
   pound; 1 slice 3½x3x½ inches ...142
   sponge, no icing; 1/12 cake 131
   yellow, chocolate icing; 1/12 cake....365
   white, no icing; 1/12 cake...........256
CANDY
   caramel; 1 ounce (3 medium)........113
   choclate bar, milk; 1 ounce 147
   chocolate fudge;
     1 piece (1 cubic inch)................84
   gumdrops; 1 ounce
     (2½ large or 20 small) 98
   hard; 1 ounce..............................109
   jelly beans; 1 ounce (10 pieces)....104
   peanut brittle; 1 ounce..................119
CANTALOUPE (muskmelon)
   ¼ (5-inch diameter).........................41
CARROT
   cooked, diced; ½ cup..................22
   raw; 1 large or 2 small..................30
CATSUP; 1 tablespoon................16
CAULIFLOWER
   cooked; ½ cup..............................14
   raw, whole flowerets; 1 cup 27
CELERY, raw, chopped; ½ cup........10
CEREAL, cooked
   oatmeal; ½ cup...........................66
   wheat, rolled; ½ cup 90

CEREAL, ready-to-eat
bran flakes; ½ cup 53
cornflakes; ½ cup 47
oats, puffed; ½ cup 50
rice, crisp cereal with
  sugar; ½ cup 70
rice, puffed; ½ cup..........................30
wheat flakes; ½ cup 53
wheat, puffed; ½ cup......................27

CHEESE
American, process; 1 ounce..........105
blue; 1 ounce 104
brick; 1 ounce 105
Camembert; 1 ounce 85
cheddar; 1 ounce............................113
cottage, dry; 1 cup 125
cottage, from skim milk,
  cream-style; 1 cup 223
cream cheese; 1 ounce 106
Edam; 1 ounce 105
Gruyère; 1 ounce 110
Limburger; 1 ounce 98
Neufchâtel; 1 ounce 70
Parmesan, grated; 1 tablespoon 23
spread, American; 1 ounce.............82
Swiss (natural); 1 ounce 105

CHERRIES
canned (heavy syrup),
  tart or sweet, pitted; ½ cup 104
canned (water pack),
  tart or sweet, pitted; ½ cup 52
fresh, sweet, whole; ½ cup.............41

CHEWING GUM, candy coated;
  1 piece 5

CHICKEN
dark meat, skinned, fried;
  4 ounces 249
dark meat, skinned, roasted;
  4 ounces 209
dark meat, with skin, fried;
  4 ounces 263
light meat, skinned, fried;
  4 ounces 223
light meat, skinned, roasted;
  4 ounces 206
light meat, with skin, fried;
  4 ounces 234
potpie; 1 individual
  (4½-inch diameter)....................545

CHICK-PEAS, raw; ½ cup 360
CHILI SAUCE; 1 tablespoon...............16
CHIVES, chopped; 1 tablespoon..........1
CHOCOLATE
bitter; (1 ounce) 143
semisweet; 1 ounce 144
sweet plain; 1 ounce......................150
syrup, fudge-type; 1 tablespoon 62
syrup, thin-type; 1 tablespoon 46
CLAMS, canned in liquor; ½ cup........57

COCOA, whole milk; 1 cup 243
COCOA POWDER, unsweetened;
  1 tablespoon................................14
COCONUT, shredded; ½ cup 138
COFFEE...0
COLA, carbonated beverage; 1 cup...96
COOKIES
butter thin; 1 (2¼-inch diameter) 23
chocolate chip; 1 49
cream sandwich, chocolate; 1.........49
fig bars; 1......................................50
gingersnap; 1 29
sugar; 1 (2¼-inch diameter) 35
vanilla wafer; 3................................42
CORN
cream style; ½ cup 105
sweet, cooked;
  1 ear (5x1¾ inches)....................80
whole kernel; ½ cup.......................137
CORNSTARCH; 1 tablespoon 29
CORN SYRUP; 1 tablespoon 59
CRAB MEAT, canned; ½ cup 68
CRACKERS
butter, rectangular; 1 17
cheese, round; 1.............................15
graham; 4 small squares................58
oyster; 10.......................................33
rusk; 1 38
rye wafer, crisp;
  2 (1⅞x3½ inches)........................45
saltine; 2 (2-inch square) 24
soda; 2 (2-inch square) 25
CRANBERRY JUICE COCKTAIL
bottled; 1 cup.................................164
CRANBERRY-ORANGE RELISH;
  1 cup..490
CRANBERRY SAUCE, sweetened,
  canned; 1 cup..............................404
CREAM
half-and-half; 1 tablespoon.............20
heavy or whipping;
  1 tablespoon 53
light; 1 tablespoon 32
light, whipped, unsweetened;
  1 tablespoon 22
CUCUMBER; 6 large slices (1 ounce)..4

D~G

DATES, fresh or dried,
  pitted; 10......................................219
DOUGHNUT
cake type, plain;
  1 (1½ ounces)............................164
yeast type; 1 (1½ ounces)............176
ECLAIR, with custard filling and
  chocolate icing;
  1 (5x2x1¾ inches) 239

EGG
fried; 1 large..................................99
scrambled, plain;
  made with 1 large egg...............111
poached, hard- or
  soft-cooked; 1 medium...............72
white only; 1 medium 15
whole; 1 large.................................82
whole; 1 medium............................72
yolk only; 1 medium 52
EGGPLANT, cooked,
  diced; ½ cup................................19
ENDIVE, raw; 1 cup 10
FIGS
canned, in syrup; ½ cup 109
dried; 1 large..................................52
raw; 3 small....................................96
FISH
bass, baked; 3 ounces 219
flounder, baked; 3 ounces.............171
haddock, fried; 3 ounces................141
halibut, broiled; 3 ounces...............144
herring, canned; 3 ounces.............176
herring, pickled; 3 ounces..............189
ocean perch, fried; 3 ounces.........192
salmon, broiled or baked;
  3 ounces....................................156
salmon, canned, pink; ½ cup.........155
sardines, canned, in oil,
  drained; 3 ounces......................174
swordfish, broiled; 3 ounces...........138
tuna, canned, in oil,
  drained; ½ cup 158
tuna, canned, in water,
  drained, ½ cup 126
FISH STICK, breaded; 1.....................50
FLOUR
cake, sifted; 1 cup 349
wheat, all-purpose enriched;
  1 tablespoon 28
wheat, all-purpose enriched,
  unsifted; 1 cup 455
FRANKFURTER, cooked; 1 139
FROSTING
caramel; 1 cup..........................1,224
chocolate, home recipe; 1 cup...1,034
white, boiled; 1 cup........................297
FRUIT COCKTAIL
canned, in syrup; ½ cup 97
canned, water-pack; ½ cup............45
GARLIC, peeled; 1 clove 4
GELATIN
dry, unflavored;
  1 envelope 23
dessert, plain, ready-to-serve;
  ½ cup 71
GINGER ALE; 1 cup 72
GOOSE, cooked; 3 ounces 198
GOOSEBERRIES, raw; 2 cups.........59

The Basics
Calorie Counts

GRAPEFRUIT
canned sections, in syrup;
½ cup 89
fresh; ½ medium 45
GRAPEFRUIT JUICE
fresh; 1 cup.............................96
canned, sweetened; 1 cup 133
canned, unsweetened; 1 cup.......101
frozen, sweetened,
reconstituted; 1 cup 117
frozen unsweetened,
reconstituted; 1 cup 101
GRAPES
concord, fresh; ½ cup 35
green, fresh; ½ cup 52
juice, canned; 1 cup 167
grape drink; 1 cup 135
GRIDDLE CAKE
buckwheat; 1 (4-inch diameter) 54
plain; 1 (4-inch diameter) 61

H~O

HAM, fully cooked, lean;
3 ounces 159
HONEY; 1 tablespoon..................64
HONEYDEW MELON; ¼ medium
(6½-inch diameter).....................124
HORSERADISH, prepared;
1 tablespoon.............................6
ICE CREAM, vanilla,
10 percent fat; 1 cup 257
ice milk; 1 cup 199
soft serve; 1 cup 266
JAM; 1 tablespoon 54
JELLY; 1 tablespoon 49
KALE, cooked; ½ cup 22
KOHLRABI, cooked; ½ cup 20
LAMB, cooked
loin chop, lean; 3 ounces.............159
rib chop, lean; 3 ounces.............180
roast leg, lean; 3 ounces.............158
LARD; 1 tablespoon....................117
LEMON; 1 medium.....................20
LEMONADE, frozen, sweetened,
reconstituted; 1 cup 107
LEMON JUICE; 1 tablespoon..............4
LENTILS, cooked; ½ cup 106
LETTUCE
Boston; ¼ medium head 6
iceberg; ¼ medium
compact head 18
leaves; 2 large or 4 small 10
LIME; 1 medium.........................19
LIME JUICE; 1 tablespoon 4
LIVERWURST; 2 ounces
(3¼-inch diameter, ¼ inch thick) ...175
LOBSTER, canned; ½ cup 69

LUNCHEON MEAT
bologna; 1 ounce......................79
ham, boiled; 1 ounce 66
salami cooked, 1 ounce 88
MACARONI, cooked; ½ cup.........78
MACARONI AND CHEESE,
baked; ½ cup 215
MALTED MILK; 1 cup..................244
MAPLE SYRUP; 1 tablespoon 50
MARGARINE; 1 tablespoon.............102
MARMALADE, orange; 1 tablespoon 51
MARSHMALLOWS; 1 ounce............90
MELBA TOAST; 1 slice 15
MILK
buttermilk; 1 cup 88
chocolate drink; 1 cup 190
condensed, sweetened,
undiluted; 1 cup....................982
dried nonfat,
instant, reconstituted; 1 cup........81
evaporated, undiluted; 1 cup 345
skim; 1 cup 88
skim, 2-percent fat; 1 cup............145
whole; 1 cup 159
MOLASSES, light; 1 tablespoon.........50
MUFFIN
bran; 1 (2⅝-inch diameter) 104
blueberry; 1 (2⅜-inch diameter).....112
corn; 1 (2¼-inch diameter) 126
plain; 1 (2¾-inch diameter) 118
MUSHROOMS, raw; 1 cup..............20
MUSTARD, prepared; 1 tablespoon ...12
MUSTARD GREENS, cooked;
½ cup 16
NECTARINES, raw; 1
(2½-inch diameter)..........................88
NOODLES
cooked; ½ cup 100
dry; 1 ounce...........................110
NUTS
almonds, shelled, chopped;
1 tablespoon 48
Brazil nuts; 3 89
cashews, roasted; 4 or 5.............75
peanuts, roasted, shelled,
chopped; 1 tablespoon.............52
pecans, chopped; 1 tablespoon 52
pistachio; 1 ounce...................168
walnuts, chopped; 1 tablespoon......52
OILS
corn; 1 tablespoon....................120
olive; 1 tablespoon...................119
peanut; 1 tablespoon.................119
safflower; 1 tablespoon..............120
sesame; 1 tablespoon.................120
soybean; 1 tablespoon................120
OKRA
fresh, cooked; 10 pods (3x⅝ inch) .31
frozen, cooked; ½ cup 35

OLIVES, green; 4 medium 15
OLIVES, ripe; 3 small.....................15
ONION
cooked; ½ cup.........................30
green, without tops; 6 small..........14
mature, raw; 1 medium 32
mature, raw, chopped;
1 tablespoon 4
ORANGE; 1 medium 64
ORANGE JUICE
canned, unsweetened; 1 cup.........120
fresh; 1 cup...........................112
frozen concentrate,
reconstituted; 1 cup 122
OYSTERS
fried; 1 ounce..........................68
raw; ½ cup (6 to 10 medium)..........79

P~S

PANCAKE; 1 (4-inch diameter).........61
PARSLEY, raw; 1 tablespoon.............2
PARSNIPS, cooked; ½ cup.............51
PEACHES
canned; 1 half and
2 tablespoons syrup..................96
canned (water-pack); ½ cup 35
fresh; 1 medium 38
frozen, sweetened; ½ cup 110
PEANUT BUTTER; 1 tablespoon........94
PEARS
canned; 2 halves and
2 tablespoons syrup..................91
fresh; 1 medium 100
PEAS, green, cooked; ½ cup 57
PEPPER, GREEN, sweet, chopped;
½ cup 16
PICKLE RELISH, sweet;
1 tablespoon 21
PICKLES
dill; 1 large (4x1¾ inches) 15
sweet; 1 medium (2¾x¾ inch).........30
PIE (⅙ of a 9-inch pie)
apple 404
blueberry 382
cherry 412
custard 331
lemon meringue......................357
mince.................................428
pumpkin..............................321
PIE SHELL, baked; one 9-inch 900
PIMIENTO; 2 tablespoons................7
PINEAPPLE
canned, in syrup; ½ cup..............86
canned, water-pack; ½ cup 48
fresh, diced; ½ cup 40
PIZZA, cheese; ⅛ of
14-inch pie 153

PLUMS
canned, syrup pack; ½ cup 107
canned, water-pack; ½ cup.............57
fresh; 1 (2-inch diameter) 6
POMEGRANATE, raw; 1 medium 97
POPCORN
oil and salt; 1 cup 41
plain; 1 cup 23
POPOVER, home recipe; 1............90
PORK, cooked
chop, loin center cut, lean only;
3 ounces 198
picnic shoulder, fresh, lean;
3 ounces 180
sausage, links or patty;
3 ounces 291
POTATO CHIPS; 10 medium............114
POTATOES
baked; 1 medium 145
boiled; 1 medium.........................173
french fried, homemade;
10 medium 214
french fried, frozen oven heated;
10 medium 172
hash-brown; ½ cup 177
mashed with milk; ½ cup 68
scalloped and au gratin,
with cheese; ½ cup 178
scalloped and au gratin,
without cheese; ½ cup 128
sweet, baked; 1 medium...............148
sweet, candied; 1 medium.............295
sweet, canned, vacuum packed;
½ cup.......................................108
POTATO STICKS; 1 cup.................190
PRETZELS; 10 small sticks 23
PRUNE JUICE, canned; 1 cup 197
PRUNES, dried
cooked, unsweetened; ½ cup 127
uncooked, pitted; 1 cup.................459
PUDDING, cornstarch
chocolate; ½ cup 192
vanilla; ½ cup 141
PUMPKIN, canned; 1 cup 81
RABBIT, domestic; 3 ounces 183
RADISHES, raw; 5 medium...................5
RAISINS; 1 cup 419
RASPBERRIES
black, fresh; ½ cup 49
red, canned; ½ cup 43
red, fresh; ½ cup 35
red, frozen, sweetened; ½ cup......122
RHUBARB
cooked, sweetened; ½ cup 191
raw, diced; 1 cup 20
RICE
brown, cooked; ½ cup.................116
quick-cooking, cooked; ½ cup 90
white, cooked; ½ cup...................112

RICE PRODUCTS, ready-to-eat
breakfast cereals
oven-popped, sweetened; 1 cup ...117
puffed, unsweetened; 1 cup 60
shredded, sweetened; 1 cup 98
ROLL
bun (frankfurter or
hamburger); 1.............................119
hard; 1 medium.............................156
plain; 1 medium.............................119
sweet; 1 medium...........................179
RUSK, 3¾-inch diameter,
½ inch thick; 1 38
RUTABAGAS, cooked; ½ cup............30
SALAD DRESSING
blue cheese; 1 tablespoon 76
French; 1 tablespoon......................66
home-cooked; 1 tablespoon............26
Italian; 1 tablespoon.......................83
mayonnaise; 1 tablespoon............101
mayonnaise-type; 1 tablespoon.......65
mayonnaise-type, low cal;
1 tablespoon................................22
Russian; 1 tablespoon 74
Thousand Island; 1 tablespoon.......80
SAUERKRAUT, canned; ½ cup.........21
SCALLOPS, cooked; 3 ounces..........99
SHERBET, orange; ½ cup 130
SHORTENING; 1 tablespoon............111
SHRIMP
canned; 3 ounces 100
french-fried; 3 ounces.................192
fresh, boiled; 3 ounces 98
SOUP, condensed, canned, diluted
with water unless specified
otherwise
bean with pork; 1 cup...................168
beef bouillon broth,
consommé; 1 cup..........................31
beef noodle; 1 cup.........................67
chicken noodle; 1 cup 62
clam chowder, Manhattan-
style; 1 cup....................................81
cream of asparagus, diluted
with milk; 1 cup..........................147
cream of celery, diluted
with milk; 1 cup..........................169
cream of mushroom, diluted
with milk; 1 cup..........................216
split-pea; 1 cup...........................145
tomato; 1 cup.................................88
tomato, diluted with milk; 1 cup.....173
vegetable with beef broth;
1 cup..78
SOY SAUCE; 1 tablespoon...............12
SPINACH
canned; ½ cup..............................22
frozen, chopped, cooked; ½ cup ...23
raw, torn; 1 cup 14

SQUASH
frozen, cooked; ½ cup 45
summer, cooked, diced; ½ cup.......15
winter, baked, mashed; ½ cup 65
STRAWBERRIES
fresh, whole; ½ cup 28
frozen, sweetened, whole;
½ cup...117
SUCCOTASH, frozen; ½ cup.............75
SUGAR
brown, packed; 1 tablespoon..........34
granulated; 1 tablespoon................46
powdered; 1 tablespoon.................31

T–Z

TANGERINE; 1 medium 39
TAPIOCA, granulated; 1 tablespoon...30
TARTAR SAUCE; 1 tablespoon..........74
TEA...0
TOMATO CATSUP; 1 tablespoon.......16
TOMATO CHILI SAUCE
1 tablespoon...................................16
TOMATO
canned; ½ cup..............................25
fresh; 1 medium.............................27
juice, canned; 1 cup 46
paste, canned; 6 ounces 139
purée; 1 cup 88
sauce; 1 cup.................................70
TURKEY, roasted;
3 slices (4x2x¼ inch).....................162
TURNIP GREENS, cooked; ½ cup.....15
TURNIPS, cooked, diced; ½ cup........18
VEAL, cooked
cutlet; 3 ounces 184
loin chop; 3 ounces 198
rib roast; 3½ ounces....................229
VEGETABLE JUICE COCKTAIL
1 cup..41
VEGETABLES, mixed, frozen,
cooked; ½ cup...............................58
VINEGAR; 1 tablespoon.......................2
WAFFLE; 1 (4½x4½x⅝ inch) 140
WATER CHESTNUTS; 4 55
WATERCRESS, raw, chopped;
½ cup...12
WATERMELON; 1 wedge
(8x4 inches) 111
YEAST, active, dry; 1 envelope..........20
YOGURT
low-fat fruit-flavored; ½ cup...........115
plain, made from skim milk;
½ cup...61
plain, made from whole milk;
½ cup...76
ZUCCHINI; 1 medium 26
ZWIEBACK; 1 piece.......................30

Calorie-Trimmed
Classics

Turn to this section for calorie-trimmed versions of old favorites such as (from left) *Canneloni Crepes, Sweet and Sour Pork Skillet, Orange Chiffon Cheesecake,* and *Shrimp-Cucumber Mousse.* (See index for recipe pages.)

Calorie-Trimmed Classics

Don't—even if you are a serious dieter—think you must forever forsake enjoying classic delights such as a rich beef stroganoff or a slice of cheesecake. With some artful cooking skills, you can reduce calories in classic dishes. Here are some of the techniques we use: In meat dishes we use leaner cuts of meats and less oil (or none at all!) for browning. In some recipes we substitute yogurt or skim milk for sour cream and light cream—just as tasty but with fewer calories. Serving sizes are a bit smaller, too; not much, but enough to make a difference.

NUTRITIONAL ANALYSIS

Per Serving

	CALORIES	PROTEIN gms.	CARBOHYDRATE gms.	FAT gms.	SODIUM mgs.	POTASSIUM mgs.	PROTEIN	VITAMIN A	VITAMIN C	THIAMINE	RIBOFLAVIN	NIACIN	CALCIUM	IRON
							Percent U.S. RDA Per Serving							
Asparagus in Cream Sauce (p. 21)	96	6	7	5	215	253	10	22	40	12	18	9	11	6
Beef Bourguignonne (p. 18)	240	19	21	6	113	396	29	41	7	12	16	23	3	16
Calorie-Reduced Beef Stroganoff (p. 20)	308	20	33	8	916	460	31	2	5	15	24	28	9	18
Calorie-Reduced Moussaka (p. 17)	388	28	15	21	859	577	43	14	15	14	26	28	15	24
Canneloni Crepes (p. 20)	337	24	25	15	745	560	36	84	29	18	30	19	30	20
Chicken Paprika (p. 20)	301	32	19	11	311	192	49	15	15	12	19	58	6	14
Chocolate Milk Shake (p. 22)	126	5	15	6	81	226	7	4	1	2	13	1	16	2
Dilled Scallop Salad (p. 18)	294	28	13	15	1409	876	43	19	45	12	7	11	17	23
Low-Calorie Orange Alaskas (p. 23)	108	2	21	2	13	274	4	5	110	9	4	3	5	3
Mocha Milk Shake (p. 22)	127	5	15	6	81	235	7	4	1	2	13	1	16	2
Mocha Sponge Cake (p. 23)	133	4	23	3	116	67	6	5	0	5	7	3	3	4
Mock Hollandaise Sauce (p. 20)	17	0	1	1	9	20	1	1	1	0	1	0	2	0
Mushroom Appetizer Supreme (p. 22)	115	6	12	5	331	258	10	6	6	6	17	11	14	5
Orange Chiffon Cheesecake (p. 23)	158	5	14	9	175	78	7	7	7	4	7	2	5	2
Pineapple-Stuffed Cornish Hens (p. 17)	291	40	11	9	335	130	61	11	11	11	22	75	4	16
Sherried Tomato Soup (p. 22)	97	2	14	3	793	494	3	55	57	7	4	8	3	11
Shrimp-Cucumber Mousse (p. 22)	47	6	4	1	44	133	9	4	9	2	5	2	6	4
Slim Oven Beef Stew (p. 18)	184	18	20	3	705	584	28	98	33	12	14	23	6	17
Strawberry Milk Shake (p. 22)	120	5	13	6	75	232	7	4	25	2	14	1	16	2
Stuffed Mushrooms (p. 21)	18	1	1	1	63	65	1	2	1	1	4	3	0	1
Sweet and Sour Pork Skillet (p. 17)	347	17	47	10	916	380	26	81	44	43	12	22	4	19
Veal Parmesan (p. 18)	229	22	5	13	363	263	34	11	26	5	15	19	15	13
Vichyssoise (p. 21)	168	7	20	7	525	517	10	6	27	7	16	6	19	3
Watercress-Endive-Orange Salad (p. 21)	78	2	7	5	40	275	3	52	54	6	7	3	8	8

Classics
Main Dishes

Sweet and Sour Pork Skillet
347/serving

This Oriental-style main dish, pictured on pages 14 and 15 and also on the cover, boasts lots of flavor for its moderate calorie count—

- ¾ pound boneless pork
- 1 tablespoon cooking oil
- 1 large green pepper, cut into ¾-inch pieces
- 2 medium carrots, thinly bias sliced
- 1 clove garlic, minced
- 1¼ cups water
- ¼ cup sugar
- ¼ cup red wine vinegar
- 1 tablespoon soy sauce
- 1¼ teaspoons instant chicken bouillon granules
- ¼ cup cold water
- 2 tablespoons cornstarch
- 2 cups hot cooked rice

Partially freeze pork; slice thinly across the grain into bite-size strips. In skillet over high heat, quickly cook pork strips in oil about 4 minutes or till browned. Remove pork from skillet; drain well on paper toweling.

Add green pepper, sliced carrots, and garlic to drippings in skillet; cook about 4 minutes or till vegetables are crisp-tender but not brown. Drain off fat. Stir in the 1¼ cups water, the sugar, vinegar, soy sauce, bouillon granules, and pork strips. Bring to boiling; boil rapidly for 1 minute. Blend the ¼ cup cold water into the cornstarch. Stir into vegetable and meat mixture. Cook and stir till thickened and bubbly. Serve over hot cooked rice. Makes 4 servings.

Calorie-Reduced Moussaka
388/serving

- 1 small eggplant (about 14 ounces), peeled and cut into ¼-inch slices
- ¾ pound ground lamb
- ½ cup chopped onion
- 1 clove garlic, minced
- ½ cup tomato sauce
- ⅓ cup dry red wine
- 1 tablespoon snipped parsley
  Dash ground cinnamon
- 1 beaten egg
- 4 teaspoons all-purpose flour
- ⅛ teaspoon ground cinnamon
  Dash ground nutmeg
- ¾ cup skim milk
- 1 beaten egg
- 3 tablespoons grated Parmesan cheese
  Ground cinnamon

In saucepan place eggplant slices in steamer basket over boiling water; cover and steam about 8 minutes. Drain on paper toweling. In skillet cook meat, onion, and garlic till meat is browned; drain. Stir in tomato sauce, wine, parsley, dash cinnamon, and ½ teaspoon salt. Simmer, uncovered, 8 minutes. Remove from heat. Gradually stir *half* of the hot mixture into 1 beaten egg; return all to skillet.

Meanwhile, prepare sauce. In saucepan combine flour, ⅛ teaspoon cinnamon, nutmeg, ½ teaspoon *salt*, and dash *pepper*; gradually stir in milk till smooth. Cook and stir till bubbly. Remove from heat. Gradually stir *half* of the hot sauce into 1 beaten egg; return all to pan. In 8x8x2-inch baking pan place *half* the eggplant. Pour meat mixture over eggplant; top with remaining eggplant. Pour sauce over all. Sprinkle with Parmesan and additional cinnamon. Bake in 325° oven about 30 minutes. Makes 4 servings.

Pineapple-Stuffed Cornish Hens—291/serving

- 3 1- to 1¼-pound Cornish game hens
- ½ cup quick-cooking rice
- ⅓ cup chopped onion
- ⅓ cup chopped celery
- 1 tablespoon butter *or* margarine
- 1 cup chopped fresh mushrooms
- ½ cup crushed pineapple (juice pack), drained
- 3 tablespoons snipped parsley
- ¾ teaspoon salt
- ¼ teaspoon dried marjoram, crushed
- ¼ teaspoon dried thyme, crushed
- 1 beaten egg
- 1 tablespoon butter *or* margarine, melted

Have butcher halve Cornish game hens lengthwise. Rinse poultry and pat dry. Rub cavities using salt, if desired. For stuffing, cook rice according to package directions. Cook onion and celery in 1 tablespoon butter or margarine till tender but not brown. In mixing bowl stir together cooked rice, the onion-celery mixture, mushrooms, drained pineapple, parsley, salt, marjoram, and thyme. Stir in beaten egg.

In 15x10x1-inch baking pan, place 6 equal mounds of stuffing mixture. Place each poultry half, cut side down, over one of the mounds of stuffing. Cover poultry loosely with foil. Bake in 375° oven for 30 minutes. Using a poultry baster, remove excess fat from pan. Uncover poultry; bake 30 minutes more or till done, basting occasionally with the 1 tablespoon melted butter or margarine and pan drippings. Makes 6 servings.

Main Dishes

Slick Trimming Tricks

Cooking oils and shortening, at about 120 calories per tablespoon, can slyly hamper your calorie-watching efforts if you don't keep a careful eye on them. To cut some of their calories, panfry and brown foods in small amounts of fat—or in none at all. For no additional calories in your cooking, use pots and pans with non-stick coatings, or apply a non-stick vegetable spray coating to your utensils.

Beef Bourguignonne 240/serving

- ¾ pound boneless beef round steak, cut 1 inch thick
- 1 clove garlic, minced
- 2 teaspoons cooking oil
- 2 tablespoons all-purpose flour
- 1 medium onion, sliced
- ½ cup dry red wine
- ½ teaspoon instant beef bouillon granules
- ⅛ teaspoon dried oregano, crushed
- ⅛ teaspoon dried thyme, crushed
- 1 small bay leaf
- 1 cup sliced carrot
- 1 cup sliced fresh mushrooms
- 1⅓ cups hot cooked noodles

Trim fat from beef; cut meat into 1-inch cubes. In a 2-quart saucepan cook meat, *half* at a time, and garlic in hot oil till browned. Add flour, stirring to coat meat. Add onion, wine, bouillon granules, herbs, and ¼ cup *water*. Cover and cook over low heat 40 minutes. Add carrots and mushrooms; cook 20 minutes more. Remove bay leaf. Season to taste with salt and pepper. Serve with hot noodles. Makes 4 servings.

Veal Parmesan—229/serving

- 1 pound veal leg round steak
- ½ cup chopped onion
- 1 clove garlic, minced
- 1 tablespoon butter *or* margarine
- 2 tablespoons grated Parmesan cheese
- ¼ cup chopped green pepper
- ½ cup tomato sauce
- ¼ teaspoon sugar
- ¼ teaspoon dried basil, crushed
- ½ cup shredded mozzarella cheese

Cut veal into 4 pieces; pound with meat mallet to ¼-inch thickness. In skillet cook onion and garlic in butter till almost tender. Push to one side of skillet; add meat to skillet and brown on both sides. Sprinkle with Parmesan; add green pepper. Combine tomato sauce, sugar, and basil. Pour over meat, stirring in the onion mixture; cover and cook over low heat for 20 to 25 minutes or till meat is tender. Sprinkle mozzarella over meat. Cover and cook 1 to 2 minutes more to melt cheese. Skim fat from remaining juices; pass juices with meat. Serves 4.

Slim Oven Beef Stew 184/serving

- ¾ pound lean boneless beef, cut into ¾-inch cubes
- 2 medium carrots, cut into ¾-inch pieces
- 1 potato, peeled and quartered
- 1 stalk celery, sliced
- 1 8-ounce can tomato sauce
- 1 tablespoon *regular* dry onion soup mix
- 1 tablespoon quick-cooking tapioca
- 1 teaspoon instant beef bouillon granules
- ½ teaspoon dried thyme, crushed
- 1 9-ounce package frozen cut green beans, thawed

In 2-quart casserole combine beef cubes, carrots, potato, and celery. In a mixing bowl combine tomato sauce, dry soup mix, tapioca, bouillon granules, thyme, and ¼ cup *water*; stir into meat mixture. Cover and bake in 325° oven for 1 hour. Stir in beans; cover and bake about 45 minutes more or till meat and vegetables are tender. Makes 4 servings.

Dilled Scallop Salad 294/serving

- ½ pound fresh *or* frozen scallops
- 1 medium tomato, seeded and chopped
- ½ cup chopped celery
- 2 tablespoons sliced green onion
- 1 tablespoon snipped fresh dillweed *or* 1 teaspoon dried dillweed
- 2 tablespoons dry white wine
- 2 tablespoons lemon *or* lime juice
- 2 tablespoons cooking oil
- 1 teaspoon sugar
  Lettuce

Thaw scallops, if frozen. Cut large scallops in half. Heat 1 cup *water* and ½ teaspoon *salt* to boiling; add scallops. Reduce heat; simmer for 1 minute or till scallops are opaque. Drain; cool. Combine cooled scallops, tomato, celery, onion, and dillweed. For dressing, in screw-top jar combine wine, fruit juice, oil, sugar, ½ teaspoon *salt*, and dash *pepper*. Cover and shake well. Pour over scallop mixture; toss to coat. Chill. To serve, drain mixture and spoon onto a lettuce-lined plate. Serves 2.

Dilled Scallop Salad and *Watercress-Endive-Orange Salad* (see recipe, page 21) are a cool change of pace for calorie-watchers.

Canneloni Crepes
337/serving

pictured on pages 14 and 15

- 8 Calorie Counter's Crepes (see recipe, right)
- ½ of a 10-ounce package frozen chopped spinach
- ½ pound lean ground beef *or* ground pork
- ¼ cup chopped onion
- ¼ cup chopped celery
- ¼ cup shredded carrot
- 1 small clove garlic, minced
- 2 tablespoons grated Parmesan cheese
- 2 tablespoons dry white wine
- 2 tablespoons tomato paste
- 1 beaten egg
- ½ teaspoon dried basil, crushed
- ¼ teaspoon dried oregano, crushed
- ½ cup cold skim milk
- 2 tablespoons all-purpose flour
- ½ teaspoon instant chicken bouillon granules
  Dash white pepper
- ½ cup shredded mozzarella cheese (2 ounces)

Prepare Calorie Counter's Crepes; set aside. Cook frozen spinach according to package directions. Drain well, squeezing out excess liquid. Set aside. For filling, in skillet cook meat, onion, celery, carrot, and garlic till meat is browned and vegetables are tender; drain. Stir in spinach, Parmesan cheese, wine, tomato paste, beaten egg, basil, oregano, and ½ teaspoon *salt*.

For sauce, in saucepan gradually stir cold milk into flour till smooth. Add bouillon granules, white pepper, ½ cup *water*, and ¼ teaspoon *salt*. Cook and stir till thickened and bubbly. Remove from heat.

To assemble crepes, spoon about ¼ cup filling down center of unbrowned side of each crepe; roll up. Place filled crepes, seam side down, in 12x7½x2-inch baking dish. Pour sauce over all. Cover; bake in 375°

oven about 20 minutes. Sprinkle with mozzarella; bake, uncovered, 3 minutes. Serves 4.

Calorie Counter's Crepes: In bowl combine 1 cup all-purpose *flour*, 1½ cups skim *milk*, 1 *egg*, and ¼ teaspoon *salt*; beat with a rotary beater till blended. Heat a lightly greased 6-inch skillet. Remove from heat; spoon in about 2 tablespoons batter. Lift and tilt skillet to spread batter. Return to heat; brown on one side only. Invert pan over paper toweling; remove crepe. Repeat to make about 18 crepes, greasing skillet occasionally. To freeze, stack crepes between layers of waxed paper. Overwrap the stack in a moisture-vapor-proof bag then place in a plastic container. Freeze up to 4 months. Thaw before using. (42/crepe)

Chicken Paprika
301/serving

- 2 whole medium chicken breasts (about 1½ pounds), split and skinned
- 2 tablespoons butter *or* margarine
- 1 small onion, thinly sliced
- ¾ cup tomato juice
- 1 tablespoon paprika
- 1 tablespoon cornstarch
- ½ cup plain yogurt
- 1⅓ cups hot cooked noodles

In skillet, over medium heat, brown chicken in butter about 15 minutes total. Remove chicken; drain on paper toweling. Add onion to skillet; cook till tender. Drain. Stir tomato juice, paprika, ¼ teaspoon *salt*, and dash *pepper* into skillet. Add chicken. Cover; simmer for 35 to 40 minutes or till tender. Remove chicken to platter; keep warm. Skim fat from pan juices. Stir cornstarch into yogurt. Stir ½ cup pan juices into yogurt mixture; return all to skillet. Cook and stir till thickened; *do not boil*. Serve chicken and sauce with noodles. Serves 4.

Calorie-Reduced Beef
Stroganoff—308/serving

- ¾ pound beef round steak, cut ½ inch thick
- 1 tablespoon cooking oil
- 2 cups sliced fresh mushrooms
- ½ cup dry sherry
- ½ teaspoon instant beef bouillon granules
- 1 8-ounce carton plain yogurt
- 1 tablespoon all-purpose flour
- 1 teaspoon sugar
- 2 cups hot cooked rice

Trim fat from round steak. Partially freeze steak. Thinly slice across grain into bite-size strips. In skillet brown meat, *half* at a time, in hot oil for 2 to 4 minutes. Remove meat from skillet. Add sliced mushrooms to skillet; cook for 2 to 3 minutes or till tender. Remove mushrooms. Add sherry, bouillon granules, and ½ cup *water* to skillet; bring to boiling. Cook, uncovered, over high heat about 3 minutes or till liquid is reduced to ⅓ cup. Combine yogurt, flour, sugar, ¾ teaspoon *salt*, and dash *pepper*; mix well. Stir yogurt mixture into liquid in skillet; stir in meat and mushrooms. Cook and stir over low heat till thickened and heated through; *do not boil*. Serve over hot cooked rice. Sprinkle with snipped parsley, if desired. Makes 4 servings.

Mock Hollandaise Sauce
17/tablespoon

- ¼ cup dairy sour cream
- ¼ cup plain yogurt
- 1 teaspoon lemon juice
- ½ teaspoon prepared mustard

In small saucepan combine all ingredients. Cook and stir over very low heat till heated through; *do not boil*. Serve over poultry, fish, and cooked vegetables. Makes ½ cup sauce.

Classics
Side Dishes

Asparagus in Cream Sauce
96/serving

¾ pound fresh asparagus *or* one
    8-ounce package frozen cut
    asparagus
1½ teaspoons butter *or* margarine
1 tablespoon all-purpose flour
¼ teaspoon salt
    Dash ground nutmeg
½ cup skim milk
¼ cup shredded Swiss *or*
    cheddar cheese (1 ounce)
1 2½-ounce jar sliced
    mushrooms, drained
1 hard-cooked egg, chopped
2 tablespoons crushed saltine
    crackers (about 3 crackers)
1 teaspoon butter *or*
    margarine, melted

For fresh asparagus, wash and scrape off scales. Break off woody bases at point where spears snap easily. Cut spears into 1-inch pieces. In covered saucepan cook cut-up fresh asparagus in small amount of boiling salted water for 8 to 10 minutes or till crisp-tender. (*Or*, cook frozen asparagus according to package directions.) Drain asparagus.

For sauce, in small saucepan melt the 1½ teaspoons butter or margarine. Blend in flour, salt, and nutmeg. Add milk all at once. Cook and stir till thickened and bubbly. Reduce heat; add cheese, stirring to melt.

In 1-quart casserole combine cooked and drained asparagus, the sliced mushrooms, and chopped egg. Gently fold in cheese sauce. Combine cracker crumbs and the 1 teaspoon melted butter or margarine; sprinkle over mixture in casserole. Bake in 350° oven for 20 minutes or till heated through. Makes 5 servings.

Microwave directions: For fresh asparagus, break off ends; cut into 1-inch pieces. Combine asparagus and ¼ cup *water* in a 1-quart non-metal casserole. Cover and cook in counter-top microwave oven on high power for 3 to 4 minutes, rearranging

once. (*Or*, place the unwrapped frozen asparagus in a 1-quart non-metal casserole. Micro-cook 6 minutes, turning after 3 minutes.) Drain asparagus. In a 2-cup glass measure micro-melt the 1½ teaspoons butter for 30 seconds. Blend in flour, salt, and nutmeg; add milk all at once, stirring well. Micro-cook, uncovered, 1 minute. Stir. Micro-cook 2 minutes or till thickened and bubbly, stirring every 30 seconds. Add cheese; stir to melt. In the casserole combine asparagus, mushrooms, and chopped egg. Gently fold in cheese sauce. Combine cracker crumbs and the 1 teaspoon melted butter or margarine; sprinkle atop. Micro-cook, covered, about 1½ minutes or till heated through.

Vichyssoise – 168/serving

2 leeks
1 small onion, sliced
1 tablespoon butter *or* margarine
2½ cups peeled and sliced
    potatoes
1 tablespoon instant chicken
    bouillon granules
1 13-ounce can evaporated
    skimmed milk

Remove tops from leeks; slice leeks (should yield about ⅔ cup). In 2-quart saucepan cook leeks and onion in butter till tender but not brown. Stir in potatoes, bouillon granules, 2⅔ cups *water*, and ½ teaspoon *salt*. Bring to boiling. Reduce heat; cover and simmer for 30 to 40 minutes or till potatoes are very tender .

In blender container or food processor bowl process potato mixture, *half* at a time, till smooth. Pour into a 2-quart bowl. Stir in evaporated skimmed milk. Season to taste with *salt* and *pepper*. Cool. Cover; chill thoroughly before serving. Garnish with snipped chives, if desired. Serves 6.

Watercress-Endive-Orange Salad—78/serving
pictured on page 19

2 tablespoons salad oil
4 teaspoons cider vinegar
1 tablespoon olive oil
1 tablespoon Dijon-style
    mustard
½ teaspoon honey
1 large bunch watercress *or*
    Bibb lettuce, torn (about
    3 cups leaves)
3 heads Belgian endive, cut
    diagonally into thin strips
2 medium oranges, peeled and
    thinly sliced

For dressing, in screw-top jar combine salad oil, vinegar, olive oil, mustard, and honey. Cover; shake well. On individual plates arrange watercress or Bibb lettuce, endive, and orange slices. Drizzle dressing over salad. Garnish with snipped parsley, if desired. Makes 6 servings.

Stuffed Mushrooms
18/appetizer

16 large fresh mushrooms
2 tablespoons sliced green onion
2 teaspoons butter *or* margarine
2 ounces Neufchâtel cheese
1½ teaspoons prepared mustard
½ teaspoon Worcestershire
    sauce

Remove stems from mushrooms; chop stems. Set mushroom caps aside. Cook chopped stems and onion in butter or margarine till vegetables are tender and liquid is absorbed. Remove from heat. Combine Neufchâtel cheese, mustard, Worcestershire, and ¼ teaspoon *salt*. Add cooked mushroom mixture; mix well. Fill mushroom caps with mixture. Place on a baking sheet; bake in 375° oven for 8 to 10 minutes or till tender. Drain on paper toweling. Makes 16 appetizers.

Classics

Side Dishes

Shrimp-Cucumber Mousse
47/serving

This refreshing side dish is pictured on pages 14 and 15—

- ¼ cup evaporated skimmed milk
- 1 envelope unflavored gelatin
- 1 cup cold water
- ½ cup plain yogurt
- 1 tablespoon lemon juice
- 2 teaspoons prepared horseradish
- 1 teaspoon sugar
- ¼ teaspoon onion juice
- ⅛ teaspoon paprika
  Dash salt
- ½ cup chopped seeded cucumber
- 1 tablespoon chopped pimiento
- 1 4½-ounce can shrimp, drained
  Lettuce

Pour evaporated skimmed milk into a small bowl; freeze till ice crystals form around edges.

Meanwhile, in saucepan soften gelatin in the cold water; heat, stirring constantly, till gelatin dissolves. Remove from heat. Cool slightly. Beat in plain yogurt, lemon juice, horseradish, sugar, onion juice, paprika, and salt. Chill mixture till partially set. (Gelatin is partially set when it has the consistency of unbeaten egg whites.) Fold chopped cucumber and pimiento into gelatin.

On high speed of electric mixer beat icy milk till soft peaks form (the tips of the peaks will bend over in soft curls when beaters are removed). Fold the beaten milk into gelatin mixture. Reserve 8 of the shrimp; fold remainder into gelatin. Turn mixture into 8 individual molds. Chill till firm. At serving time, unmold and serve on lettuce. Garnish with the reserved shrimp. Makes 8 servings.

Mushroom Appetizer
Supreme—115/serving

- ½ pound fresh mushrooms, sliced
- 1 tablespoon butter *or* margarine
- 2 tablespoons all-purpose flour
- ¼ teaspoon salt
- ¼ teaspoon instant chicken bouillon granules
  Dash pepper
- ¾ cup skim milk
- ¼ cup water
- ½ cup shredded process Swiss cheese (2 ounces)
- 2 tablespoons snipped parsley
- 1 tablespoon dry white wine
- 3 slices whole wheat bread, toasted and cut diagonally into quarters

In saucepan cook mushrooms in butter or margarine about 5 minutes or till tender. Stir in flour, salt, bouillon granules, and pepper. Add milk and water all at once; cook and stir till thickened and bubbly. Add cheese, stirring to melt. Stir in parsley and wine.

To serve, place 2 toast quarters on each plate. Top with the mushroom mixture. Makes 6 appetizer servings.

Sherried Tomato Soup
97/serving

- ⅓ cup chopped onion
- ⅓ cup shredded carrot
- 1 tablespoon butter *or* margarine
- 4 teaspoons cornstarch
- 1 teaspoon instant beef bouillon granules
  Dash ground nutmeg
- 3 cups tomato juice
- ¼ cup dry sherry
- 2 tablespoons snipped parsley
- 1 teaspoon sugar

In saucepan cook onion and carrot in butter or margarine till tender but not brown. Blend in cornstarch, bouillon granules, nutmeg, and ½ teaspoon *salt*. Add tomato juice and 1 cup *water* all at once. Cook and stir till mixture is thickened and bubbly. Stir in sherry, snipped parsley, and sugar; simmer, uncovered, for 5 minutes. Makes 4 servings.

Chocolate Milk Shake
126/serving

A rich, creamy drink that is surprisingly low in calories—

- ¾ cup evaporated skimmed milk
- ¼ cup cold water
- 2 tablespoons frozen whipped dessert topping, thawed
- 2 tablespoons chocolate-flavored syrup
- 1 teaspoon vanilla
- 6 1¼-inch ice cubes

In blender container combine evaporated skimmed milk, water, whipped dessert topping, chocolate-flavored syrup, and vanilla. Cover container. With blender running, add ice cubes one at a time through hole in lid, blending at lowest speed till thickened. Makes three 8-ounce servings.

Mocha Milk Shake: Prepare Chocolate Milk Shake as above *except* stir 1 teaspoon *instant coffee crystals* into the cold water. 127/serving.

Strawberry Milk Shake: Prepare Chocolate Milk Shake as above *except* omit chocolate-flavored syrup and add ½ cup fresh *or* frozen whole unsweetened *strawberries* and 1 tablespoon *sugar* with the evaporated skimmed milk. 120/serving.

Orange Chiffon Cheesecake
158/serving

pictured on pages 14 and 15

- 1 cup finely crushed zwieback
- 2 tablespoons sugar
- ¼ cup butter, melted
- 1 envelope unflavored gelatin
- 2 beaten egg yolks
- ½ cup skim milk
- ⅓ cup ricotta cheese
- ⅓ cup orange juice
- 2 tablespoons sugar
- 2 tablespoons orange liqueur
- 1 1½-ounce envelope dessert topping mix
- ½ cup skim milk
- 4 egg whites
  Orange slices (optional)
  Mint sprigs (optional)

Combine crushed zwieback and 2 tablespoons sugar. Add melted butter; mix till blended. Reserve 2 tablespoons of the mixture. Press remaining mixture onto bottom of a buttered 7-inch springform pan. Chill. Soften gelatin in ¼ cup *water*. In saucepan combine the egg yolks, ½ cup milk, the cheese, orange juice, 2 tablespoons sugar, the liqueur, and the softened gelatin. Cook and stir over medium heat about 20 minutes or till gelatin is dissolved and mixture coats a metal spoon; *do not boil.* Remove from heat; chill till partially set, stirring occasionally. Prepare topping mix according to package directions using the ½ cup skim milk; fold in gelatin mixture. In large bowl beat egg whites till stiff peaks form. Fold in gelatin-topping mixture. Turn into crumb-coated springform pan; cover and chill till firm. To serve, remove sides of pan and sprinkle the reserved crumb mixture atop cheesecake. Garnish platter with orange slices and mint, if desired. Makes 10 servings.

Mocha Sponge Cake
133/serving

- 1 tablespoon instant coffee crystals
- 6 egg yolks
- 1 teaspoon vanilla
- 1 cup sugar
- 6 egg whites
- ¾ teaspoon cream of tartar
- 1¼ cups all-purpose flour
- 3 tablespoons unsweetened cocoa powder
- 1 teaspoon baking powder
- 1 1½-ounce envelope dessert topping mix
- ½ cup skim milk
- 1 teaspoon instant coffee crystals

Dissolve 1 tablespoon coffee crystals in 3 tablespoons *hot water*; set aside. Beat egg yolks at high speed of electric mixer till thick and lemon-colored. Add dissolved coffee and the vanilla, beating at low speed till blended. Beat at medium speed till slightly thickened. Gradually add ½ *cup* of the sugar, beating till dissolved. Set aside. Wash beaters. In large bowl beat egg whites and cream of tartar with electric mixer to soft peaks. Gradually add the remaining ½ cup sugar, beating to stiff peaks. Carefully fold in yolk mixture. Thoroughly stir together flour, cocoa powder, baking powder, and ½ teaspoon *salt*. Carefully fold dry ingredients, one-fourth at a time, into egg white mixture. Turn into an ungreased 10-inch tube pan. Bake in 325° oven for 45 to 50 minutes or till done. Invert cake in pan; cool completely. Using a spatula, loosen cake from pan; invert onto serving plate. Beat together to soft peaks using an electric mixer the dessert topping mix, milk, and 1 teaspoon coffee crystals. Frost top and sides of cake with mixture. Refrigerate to store. Makes 16 servings.

Low-Calorie Orange
Alaskas—108/serving

Cut the hollowed-out orange tops into julienne strips. Twist and use to garnish each serving —

- 4 medium oranges
- ⅓ of a 4-ounce carton frozen whipped dessert topping, thawed
- 1 egg white
- ¼ teaspoon vanilla
- ⅛ teaspoon cream of tartar
- 1 tablespoon sugar

Cut a very thin slice off bottom of each orange to make a flat base. Cut off tops of oranges a fourth of the way down; remove tops. Carefully scoop out pulp from tops and bottoms, reserving pulp, juice, and bottom shells. Set aside top shells for garnish.

Place orange pulp and juice in blender container or food processor bowl. Cover; process till smooth. Fold in thawed whipped dessert topping. Pour mixture into a shallow pan; cover and freeze several hours or till firm.

Before serving, break up frozen orange mixture; spoon into orange shell bottoms. Place shells in freezer. In small mixer bowl beat on high speed of electric mixer the egg white with vanilla and cream of tartar till soft peaks form; gradually add sugar, beating to stiff peaks. Remove oranges from freezer. Cover tops of oranges with meringue, sealing to edges of oranges all around. Place in an 8x8x2-inch baking pan. Bake in 500° oven for 1½ to 2 minutes or till lightly browned. Serve immediately. Makes 4 servings.

Calorie-Trimmed
Main Dishes

Meats, poultry, fish, seafood, eggs, and cheese are easily prepared in this section for low-calorie eating. Pictured (from left): *Poached Halibut with Spinach, Stir-Fried Beef and Vegetables, Shrimp Stack-Ups, Vegetable-Filled Omelet,* and *Pork Turnover.* (See index for recipe pages.)

Main Dishes

The cornerstones of good diets are main dishes. Because they provide most of your daily protein requirements and contribute most of the calories in a meal, you need to carefully plan and prepare all your main dishes — whether for breakfast, lunch, or dinner.

Main dishes need to be more than nutritionally sound, however; they need to be delicious, too.

And, low-calorie main dishes need to be especially good tasting because the most nutritious low-calorie main dish is useless if it goes uneaten. The secret to successful calorie trimming is to combine nutritional knowledge and low-calorie cooking techniques to create delicious, appealing meals. In this chapter we show you how to do just that.

NUTRITIONAL ANALYSIS

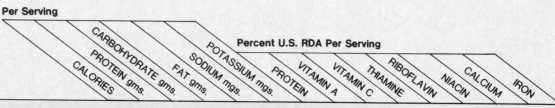

MEAT	CALORIES	PROTEIN gms.	CARBOHYDRATE gms.	FAT gms.	SODIUM mgs.	POTASSIUM mgs.	PROTEIN	VITAMIN A	VITAMIN C	THIAMINE	RIBOFLAVIN	NIACIN	CALCIUM	IRON
Apple Ham Slice (p. 38)	252	21	17	11	792	371	32	6	6	33	12	19	2	18
Barbecued Beef and Beans (p. 34)	250	26	17	9	545	458	40	17	6	8	15	21	15	22
Beefy Tossed Salad (p. 32)	173	19	8	8	147	601	30	32	98	11	17	17	17	19
Belgian Lamb Stew (p. 40)	242	19	19	10	605	685	30	22	65	12	17	24	7	14
Chinese Veal Steak (p. 31)	223	23	4	12	454	319	35	1	5	5	15	23	2	17
Creamy Lamb Crepes (p. 42)	275	16	18	14	424	237	24	10	3	12	19	12	16	7
Curried Yogurt Kebabs (p. 41)	215	23	18	5	262	796	36	8	35	16	29	35	8	13
Deluxe Beef Patties (p. 32)	306	23	7	20	500	441	35	19	42	10	15	26	3	20
Dilled Cabbage Rolls (p. 36)	244	14	17	13	628	277	21	6	17	20	15	14	8	12
Festive Pork Roast (p. 35)	177	18	4	9	135	227	28	1	1	45	12	20	1	14
Glazed Ham Kebabs (p. 40)	209	15	25	5	500	438	24	115	41	27	11	15	4	15
Grilled Beef Kebabs (p. 31)	240	24	14	8	738	321	37	3	55	7	12	19	3	20
Ham and Cheese Casserole (p. 38)	293	22	16	16	815	491	34	142	37	30	25	19	29	16
Ham and Cottage Cheese Mold (p. 38)	128	16	5	5	252	271	24	7	20	14	15	9	10	7
Ham Stew (p. 40)	159	15	17	4	282	543	22	112	47	26	12	19	4	18
Ham with Pineapple Sauce (p. 40)	165	18	5	7	664	268	28	2	18	31	10	17	2	14
Herbed Lamb Stew (p. 42)	249	19	22	10	269	782	29	85	82	15	16	25	6	13
Italian Pot Roast (p. 30)	221	29	7	8	619	240	44	15	8	7	14	26	1	21
Lamb Zucchini Casserole (p. 41)	176	18	6	9	390	449	28	117	46	9	19	12	29	13
Liver Kebabs (p. 30)	307	33	16	12	868	865	50	1228	110	26	288	102	6	62
Luau Burgers (p. 29)	390	22	17	25	649	430	34	8	23	12	15	28	3	22
Marinated Chuck Steak (p. 31)	198	21	4	11	303	190	32	0	0	3	11	17	1	16
Marinated Lamb Kebabs (p. 41)	137	14	7	6	272	521	22	7	44	11	23	26	4	9
Mexican Meatball Soup (p. 29)	281	17	14	17	1219	458	26	30	38	11	12	22	3	17
Mint-Glazed Lamb Chops (p. 41)	109	14	4	4	171	155	21	0	1	5	8	15	1	7
Minute Steak au Poivre (p. 29)	307	23	0	20	150	368	35	5	0	7	12	28	2	19
Onion Braised Lamb Chops (p. 42)	228	22	5	13	190	323	34	0	5	9	16	23	5	9
Orange Beef Stew (p. 30)	262	24	12	13	503	445	37	120	15	6	13	20	6	21

	CALORIES	PROTEIN gms.	CARBOHYDRATE gms.	FAT gms.	SODIUM mgs.	POTASSIUM mgs.	PROTEIN	VITAMIN A	VITAMIN C	THIAMINE	RIBOFLAVIN	NIACIN	CALCIUM	IRON
Orange-Ginger Ham Grill (p. 38)	332	17	14	23	875	373	27	1	23	51	12	21	2	15
Orange-Sauced Lamb Chops (p. 42)	134	14	10	4	35	284	22	2	41	8	9	16	1	6
Orange-Sauced Pork Chops (p. 35)	180	13	9	10	166	239	20	2	35	34	9	15	1	10
Oriental Pork Chops (p. 35)	193	18	5	11	424	308	28	1	5	43	14	21	2	14
Pork Turnover (p. 36)	343	15	32	17	650	258	23	3	29	38	17	19	8	15
Sauerkraut and Pork Skillet (p. 36)	220	17	12	12	682	348	26	1	18	42	13	19	4	15
Spiced Pot Roast (p. 32)	186	24	5	7	202	318	37	40	6	4	13	18	4	17
Spicy Ham Patties with Apple Rings (p. 39)	275	25	20	10	716	406	38	5	4	36	20	20	8	20
Spicy Pork Skillet (p. 36)	283	19	26	13	833	353	29	36	78	39	17	24	7	17
Spinach-Filled Beef Rolls (p. 29)	199	20	10	9	391	627	31	139	55	10	17	19	15	23
Steak-Tomato Stew (p. 35)	240	23	17	9	349	747	36	174	66	11	14	25	6	20
Stir-Fried Beef and Vegetables (p. 30)	183	20	12	7	1200	913	31	195	83	12	25	23	12	31
Tarragon Beef and Noodles (p. 31)	310	22	30	10	252	268	34	4	4	23	19	26	2	19
Veal Chops with Lemon Sauce (p. 34)	219	20	5	13	477	315	30	3	5	5	18	21	6	13
Veal Stew (p. 34)	296	19	23	14	706	519	29	24	92	15	14	26	4	18
Wine-Sauced Pot Roast (p. 34)	238	31	14	7	259	739	47	91	41	11	26	32	5	26
Yogurt Beefwiches (p. 32)	295	18	24	14	672	300	27	10	33	14	18	18	16	14
Yogurt-Sauced Pork Balls (p. 39)	264	21	12	15	673	288	32	5	3	28	17	19	6	15
POULTRY														
Chicken and Pea Pods (p. 46)	247	34	14	6	2111	241	53	18	30	23	22	62	6	27
Chicken-Cauliflower Casseroles (p. 48)	249	24	16	10	927	570	37	15	94	8	25	23	37	8
Chicken in Wine Sauce (p. 50)	267	29	7	12	631	76	44	20	15	7	14	56	3	11
Chicken Livers Tarragon (p. 51)	248	32	11	8	455	377	50	285	48	16	185	69	7	55
Chicken Veronique (p. 43)	218	28	9	6	67	98	44	5	27	6	14	54	3	11
Claypot Chicken (p. 47)	160	24	0	6	89	4	37	19	2	6	29	36	2	14
Creamy Chicken Salad (p. 47)	282	28	12	13	640	708	42	75	21	8	21	34	29	9
Curry-Sauced Chicken (p. 46)	171	29	5	3	220	78	44	4	4	5	17	56	2	10
Elegant Chicken Crepes (p. 44)	278	26	21	10	530	490	40	32	58	13	29	27	31	11
Fruited Barbecue Chicken (p. 47)	237	25	16	8	267	103	38	29	25	10	30	38	4	17
Garden Chicken Salad (p. 48)	183	25	12	4	252	627	39	19	57	10	17	33	11	15
Hawaiian Chicken (p. 50)	307	31	40	4	1174	394	47	16	92	17	18	55	11	19
Herbed Tomato Chicken (p. 47)	185	29	7	3	569	170	45	13	31	8	16	57	3	12
Lemon Chicken Breasts (p. 50)	221	30	4	9	294	146	45	9	7	7	21	58	5	10
Mandarin Chicken (p. 51)	282	27	17	12	1404	337	42	5	46	8	16	50	7	16
Plum-Sauced Chicken (p. 43)	236	24	17	6	451	88	38	20	18	7	30	36	3	16
Quick Chicken Vegetable Soup (p. 44)	155	19	15	2	573	754	30	142	86	9	9	37	5	11
Sauced Chicken over Rusks (p. 47)	236	25	24	4	406	572	38	6	13	7	21	38	14	8
Spicy Turkey Drumsticks (p. 46)	259	35	6	10	191	638	54	19	42	6	17	26	3	17
Stir-Fried Chicken with Almonds (p. 51)	357	36	19	15	707	533	55	21	48	26	35	73	8	25
Three-Cheese Chicken Bake (p. 44)	318	23	22	15	656	288	35	19	36	17	23	21	24	10
Tomato-Broccoli Chicken (p. 43)	244	31	9	9	486	416	48	60	121	12	20	59	8	15
Turkey-Fruit Salad (p. 48)	238	24	28	5	216	1081	36	185	138	18	26	27	19	28
Turkey Loaf (p. 46)	184	26	5	6	411	355	40	27	13	5	12	31	2	11

Calorie-Trimmed
Main Dishes

Percent U.S. RDA Per Serving

	CALORIES	PROTEIN gms.	CARBOHYDRATE gms.	FAT gms.	SODIUM mgs.	POTASSIUM mgs.	PROTEIN	VITAMIN A	VITAMIN C	THIAMINE	RIBOFLAVIN	NIACIN	CALCIUM	IRON
Turkey-Vegetable Bake (p. 51)	142	16	6	6	302	395	25	48	35	5	14	17	9	8
Vegetable-Stuffed Chicken Breasts (p. 48)	260	30	6	12	349	307	47	16	18	9	27	64	5	12
Wine-Sauced Chicken Livers (p. 44)	179	22	9	5	339	269	34	191	54	11	128	47	7	38
FISH & SEAFOOD														
Baked Curried Fish (p. 54)	184	19	9	8	483	443	29	3	11	4	6	15	7	7
Baked Red Snapper (p. 53)	162	32	3	1	181	655	49	5	26	20	3	2	4	9
Creamed Crab with Tomato (p. 57)	280	21	21	12	1222	451	33	29	22	11	28	12	43	8
Grapefruit-Sole Salad (p. 53)	178	14	23	4	581	566	21	14	98	9	7	14	7	10
Main Dish Tuna Toss (p. 52)	167	19	10	6	574	498	30	19	37	10	16	34	10	13
Marinated Sole (p. 54)	173	18	11	6	329	390	28	3	17	4	5	15	5	7
Marinated Tuna and Vegetables (p. 52)	245	28	33	1	878	1092	43	189	240	38	22	61	11	30
Newburg-Style Crab (p. 57)	278	15	25	12	807	320	24	28	19	20	20	11	18	12
Oriental Scallops (p. 57)	120	21	8	1	889	632	33	14	66	9	7	8	12	19
Poached Halibut with Spinach (p. 54)	268	36	6	11	398	994	56	131	53	9	15	54	18	15
Rice-Vegetable Stuffed Fish (p. 54)	305	23	13	17	678	516	36	92	15	16	13	22	5	7
Salmon-Cauliflower Casserole (p. 52)	222	18	11	12	1023	512	28	8	73	5	18	28	27	8
Salmon-Stuffed Tomatoes (p. 52)	273	21	18	15	493	1003	33	47	83	15	24	35	25	15
Shrimp and Pepper Stir-Fry (p. 57)	226	18	21	8	659	292	28	7	49	8	4	18	7	13
Shrimp Kebabs (p. 56)	169	23	12	3	435	488	36	12	40	8	4	22	9	13
Shrimp Stack-Ups (p. 56)	176	15	20	4	280	327	23	15	21	11	12	13	10	13
Spicy Shrimp Skillet (p. 56)	209	24	12	8	437	461	36	5	20	5	6	20	11	15
Vegetable-Sauced Fish Fillets (p. 53)	193	18	9	8	467	437	28	10	20	4	4	16	5	8
Vegetable-Topped Halibut Steaks (p. 56)	272	36	9	10	745	1060	55	156	40	9	9	60	6	11
Wild Rice Shrimp Creole (p. 57)	229	19	27	5	594	533	29	28	57	13	5	22	7	16
EGGS & CHEESE														
Broccoli-Yogurt Omelet (p. 60)	237	13	6	18	572	279	21	54	60	9	21	2	11	13
Cheese-Cauliflower Chowder (p. 61)	266	17	12	17	1017	371	27	18	83	5	25	5	47	7
Cheese Soufflé (p. 60)	282	17	8	20	501	180	26	26	4	6	23	1	35	9
Cheesy Strata (p. 60)	208	13	15	11	801	235	20	13	1	9	25	3	28	8
Crab and Egg Casserole (p. 60)	233	19	5	15	819	287	29	29	3	8	22	4	15	10
Egg Salad Stuffed Tomatoes (p. 61)	184	15	9	9	440	504	24	46	57	12	23	5	12	15
Individual Crustless Quiches (p. 61)	225	22	7	12	1293	264	33	14	3	7	26	5	34	13
Poached Eggs with Cheese Sauce (p. 61)	197	13	10	12	498	186	20	18	1	8	19	4	18	11
Spicy Poached Egg Stacks (p. 58)	271	16	21	14	944	333	24	20	9	27	19	13	7	16
Taco Scrambled Eggs (p. 58)	287	17	10	20	583	422	26	52	48	11	27	4	25	14
Vegetable-Filled Omelet (p. 58)	246	15	8	18	802	400	22	44	52	12	24	6	8	17

Meats

Spinach-Filled Beef Rolls 199/serving

- ¾ pound boneless beef top round steak, cut ½ inch thick
- 1 10-ounce package frozen chopped spinach, cooked and drained
- ¼ cup shredded carrot
- ¼ cup shredded sharp cheddar cheese
- ¼ teaspoon dried oregano, crushed
- ¼ teaspoon pepper
- ½ cup chopped onion
- 1 clove garlic, minced
- 1 tablespoon cooking oil
- 1 cup tomato juice
- ½ cup water
- 1 teaspoon instant beef bouillon granules
- 1 teaspoon Worcestershire sauce
- 1 tablespoon cornstarch
- ⅓ cup cold water

Cut meat into four rectangles; pound to ⅛-inch thickness. Sprinkle with salt and pepper, if desired. Combine spinach, carrot, cheese, oregano, and pepper. Spread spinach mixture over meat. Roll up jelly-roll style. Secure with wooden picks. In skillet cook onion and garlic in hot oil till tender but not brown; push aside. Add meat rolls to skillet; brown on all sides. Drain off excess fat. To skillet add tomato juice, ½ cup water, bouillon granules, and Worcestershire sauce. Cover; simmer about 40 minutes or till meat is tender. Transfer rolls to serving platter; remove wooden picks and keep meat warm. Skim excess fat from pan drippings. Stir cornstarch into ⅓ cup cold water; stir into pan juices. Cook and stir till mixture is thick and bubbly. Cook and stir 1 to 2 minutes more. Spoon mixture over meat rolls. Makes 4 servings.

Luau Burgers—390/serving

- 1 beaten egg
- 1 8-ounce can tomato sauce
- ½ cup finely crushed saltine crackers (14 crackers)
- ½ cup chopped onion
- ⅓ cup chopped green pepper
- 2 tablespoons soy sauce
- ½ teaspoon ground ginger
- 2 pounds lean ground beef
- 1 15½-ounce can pineapple slices, drained (8 slices)
- 4 maraschino cherries, drained and halved

In bowl combine egg, tomato sauce, crushed crackers, onion, green pepper, soy sauce, and ginger. Add ground beef; mix well. Shape meat mixture into eight 4-inch patties; grill over *medium* coals for 6 to 8 minutes; turn. Top each patty with a pineapple slice and cherry half. Continue to grill 6 to 8 minutes longer or till desired doneness. Makes 8 servings.

Minute Steak au Poivre 307/serving

- 4 beef cubed steaks (about 1 pound)
- 1 to 1½ teaspoons freshly ground pepper
- 2 tablespoons butter *or* margarine
  Salt
- ¼ cup brandy

Sprinkle cubed steaks on both sides with pepper, pressing in firmly with fingers. In skillet brown steaks in butter or margarine about 1 minute on each side. Sprinkle with a little salt. Add brandy to skillet; ignite. Remove steaks to warm serving platter; pour pan drippings over steaks. Makes 4 servings.

Mexican Meatball Soup 281/serving

- 1 beaten egg
- ½ cup chopped onion
- ¼ cup cornmeal
- 1 4-ounce can green chili peppers, rinsed, seeded, and chopped
- 1 clove garlic, minced
- ¾ teaspoon salt
- ¼ teaspoon dried oregano, crushed
- ⅛ teaspoon pepper
- 1 pound lean ground beef
- 3 cups water
- 1 16-ounce can tomatoes, cut up
- 1 8-ounce can tomato sauce
- ⅓ cup chopped onion
- 1 clove garlic, minced
- 1 tablespoon sugar
- 1½ teaspoons salt
- 1½ teaspoons chili powder
- ¼ teaspoon pepper
- ¼ teaspoon dried oregano, crushed

In bowl combine egg, ½ cup chopped onion, cornmeal, *half* the chopped chili peppers, 1 clove garlic, the ¾ teaspoon salt, ¼ teaspoon oregano, and the ⅛ teaspoon pepper; add ground beef. Mix well.

Using 1 rounded teaspoonful per meatball, shape mixture into 48 meatballs; set aside. In large saucepan or Dutch oven combine water, *un-drained* tomatoes, tomato sauce, ⅓ cup onion, 1 clove garlic, sugar, 1½ teaspoons salt, chili powder, ¼ teaspoon pepper, ¼ teaspoon oregano, and the remaining chili peppers. Bring to boiling. Add meatballs. Return to boiling. Cover; reduce heat and simmer 30 minutes. Makes 6 servings.

Main Dishes
Meats

Stir-Fried Beef and Vegetables—183/serving
pictured on pages 24 and 25

- ¾ pound beef top round steak
- ½ teaspoon instant beef bouillon granules
- ⅓ cup boiling water
- 3 tablespoons soy sauce
- 1 tablespoon cooking oil
- 1 clove garlic, minced
- 1 medium onion, sliced and separated into rings
- 1 cup thinly sliced carrot
- 1 cup bias-sliced celery
- 1 cup sliced fresh mushrooms
- 6 cups torn spinach leaves

Partially freeze meat. Slice meat very thinly across the grain into bite-size strips. Dissolve beef bouillon granules in boiling water. Add soy sauce; set aside.

Preheat a wok or large skillet over high heat; add oil. Stir-fry garlic in hot oil for 30 seconds. Add onion, carrot, celery, and mushrooms. Stir-fry 2 minutes. Remove vegetables. Add *half* the meat to hot wok or skillet; stir-fry 2 minutes. Remove meat. Stir-fry remaining meat 2 minutes. Return all meat to wok. Stir soy mixture; stir into meat. Cook and stir till bubbly. Stir in cooked vegetables and the spinach. Cover and cook 1 minute. Serve immediately. Makes 4 servings.

Italian Pot Roast 221/serving

- 1 3-pound beef chuck pot roast
- 8 cloves garlic
- 2 tablespoons cooking oil
- 3 8-ounce cans tomato sauce
- 2 tablespoons vinegar
- 6 to 8 whole cloves
- 1 teaspoon ground nutmeg
- ½ teaspoon ground cinnamon
- ½ teaspoon ground allspice

Make slits in top of roast using the tip of a knife; insert garlic cloves. Sprinkle roast with salt and pepper. In large skillet brown meat on both sides in hot oil. Combine remaining ingredients; pour over meat in skillet. Cover and simmer for 1½ hours or till meat is tender. Remove meat to cutting board; keep warm. Bring juices in skillet to boiling; boil, uncovered, about 5 minutes or till liquid is reduced to 3 cups. Strain sauce. Remove garlic cloves from meat, if desired. Slice meat. Spoon some of the sauce over meat; pass remaining sauce. Makes 8 servings.

Liver Kebabs—307/serving

- 1 cup tomato juice
- 2 tablespoons minced dried onion
- 1 teaspoon salt
- 1 teaspoon dried oregano, crushed
- ⅛ teaspoon garlic powder
- 1 pound beef liver, cut into 1-inch-wide strips
- 3 medium zucchini, cut into ¾-inch chunks

In deep bowl combine tomato juice, onion, salt, oregano, garlic powder, and ⅛ teaspoon *pepper*. Add liver, stirring to coat. Let stand at room temperature 30 minutes, stirring occasionally. Meanwhile, cook zucchini in boiling unsalted water for 3 minutes or till nearly tender; drain. Lift liver from marinade, reserving marinade. On four skewers thread liver loosely, accordion-style, alternating with the zucchini. Grill over *medium-hot* coals for 4 to 5 minutes, brushing occasionally with marinade. Turn. Grill and baste 4 to 5 minutes more. (*Or*, broil 4 to 5 inches from heat for 8 to 10 minutes, basting occasionally with the marinade; turn once.) Serves 4.

Orange Beef Stew 262/serving

- 2 cups dry red wine
- ½ cup chopped onion
- 2 cloves garlic, minced
- 1 tablespoon vinegar
- 1 teaspoon salt
- ½ teaspoon dried rosemary, crushed
- ½ teaspoon dried thyme, crushed
- ½ teaspoon finely shredded orange peel
- ¼ teaspoon pepper
- 2 pounds beef stew meat, cut into 1-inch cubes
- 2 ounces salt pork
- ½ cup water
- ½ teaspoon instant beef bouillon granules
- 6 carrots, bias sliced into 1-inch pieces
- 3 medium onions, quartered
- 1 cup pitted ripe olives
- 2 tablespoons cornstarch
- 2 tablespoons cold water

Combine wine, the ½ cup onion, garlic, vinegar, salt, rosemary, thyme, orange peel, and pepper. Add beef; stir to coat. Cover and marinate at room temperature for 2 hours. Drain meat, reserving marinade; pat meat dry with paper toweling. In 4-quart Dutch oven cook salt pork till 2 to 3 tablespoons fat accumulate; discard pork. Brown meat in the hot fat. Add marinade, ½ cup water, and bouillon granules; bring to boiling. Cover; simmer 1 hour. Add carrots, quartered onions, and olives; simmer, covered, 30 to 40 minutes more or till meat and vegetables are tender. Combine cornstarch and 2 tablespoons water; add to Dutch oven. Cook and stir till bubbly. Garnish with snipped parsley, if desired. Serves 8.

Marinated Chuck Steak
198/serving

⅓ cup red wine vinegar
1 tablespoon cooking oil
1 clove garlic, minced
½ teaspoon salt
½ teaspoon dried basil, crushed
¼ teaspoon dried thyme, crushed
1½ pounds beef chuck blade
　　steak, cut 1 inch thick
4 teaspoons cornstarch
2 tablespoons cold water
1 2½-ounce jar sliced
　　mushrooms, drained
¼ teaspoon Kitchen Bouquet
　　(optional)

For marinade, combine red wine vinegar, oil, garlic, salt, basil, and thyme. Trim excess fat from meat; pierce all surfaces of meat with long-tined fork. Place meat in plastic bag; set in shallow dish. Add marinade to bag; turn bag to coat all surfaces of meat. Close bag. Refrigerate for 8 hours or overnight, turning plastic bag several times to distribute marinade. Drain meat; reserve *3 tablespoons* marinade. Add water to reserved marinade to equal 1 cup liquid. Place meat on unheated rack of broiler pan. Broil meat 4 inches from heat till desired doneness (allow 12 to 14 minutes total for medium); turn meat once halfway through cooking time.

　Meanwhile, in small saucepan stir cornstarch into cold water. Add reserved marinade mixture. Cook and stir till thickened and bubbly. Add mushrooms and Kitchen Bouquet, if desired; heat through. Season to taste with additional salt. Slice meat across the grain into thin slices. Serve with mushroom mixture. Makes 4 servings.

Grilled Beef Kebabs
240/serving

1 pound beef stew meat, cut
　　into 1-inch cubes
½ cup bottled teriyaki sauce
⅓ cup dry red wine
1 tablespoon Worcestershire
　　sauce
½ teaspoon garlic salt
　　Unseasoned instant meat
　　tenderizer
½ small pineapple
1 large green pepper, cut into
　　1-inch squares

Place meat in bowl. Mix teriyaki sauce, wine, Worcestershire sauce, and garlic salt. Pour over meat. Cover and refrigerate overnight or let stand at room temperature 2 hours, stirring occasionally. Drain meat, reserving marinade. Sprinkle meat with the tenderizer according to package directions. Remove crown from pineapple; cut off peel and remove eyes. Slice pineapple, then cut into wedges. On four skewers thread meat alternately with green pepper and pineapple. Grill over *hot* coals 8 minutes; baste with marinade. Turn; grill 7 minutes more. (*Or*, broil 4 to 5 inches from heat for 8 minutes. Turn; brush with marinade. Broil 7 minutes more.) Brush again with marinade. Makes 4 servings.

Chinese Veal Steak
223/serving

1 pound veal leg round steak
1 tablespoon cooking oil
½ cup chopped onion
½ cup water
¼ cup bias-sliced celery
1 2½-ounce jar sliced
　　mushrooms, drained
1 tablespoon soy sauce
½ teaspoon instant chicken
　　bouillon granules
2 teaspoons cornstarch

Cut veal into 4 pieces; pound with meat mallet to ¼-inch thickness. In large skillet brown veal in hot cooking oil. Drain off excess fat. Add water, onion, celery, mushrooms, soy sauce, and bouillon granules. Cover and simmer for 30 minutes or till veal is tender. Remove veal to warm serving platter. Combine cornstarch and 2 tablespoons *cold water;* stir into mixture in skillet. Cook and stir till thickened and bubbly. Pour some mushroom mixture over veal; pass remainder. Makes 4 servings.

Tarragon Beef and Noodles
310/serving

¾ pound beef stew meat, cut
　　into ¾-inch cubes
1 clove garlic, minced
1 tablespoon cooking oil
1 cup water
¼ cup red wine vinegar
1 teaspoon sugar
1 teaspoon instant beef
　　bouillon granules
½ teaspoon dried tarragon,
　　crushed
1 4-ounce can sliced
　　mushrooms, drained
¼ cup sliced green onion
1 tablespoon cornstarch
3 ounces medium noodles,
　　cooked

In large saucepan cook meat and garlic in cooking oil till meat is browned. Drain off excess fat. Add water, vinegar, sugar, beef bouillon granules, tarragon, and ¼ teaspoon *salt.* Cover and simmer for 1 to 1¼ hours or till meat is tender. Add mushrooms and green onion; simmer 10 minutes more. Measure pan juices. If necessary, add water to pan juices to measure ¾ cup liquid; return to saucepan. Combine cornstarch and ¼ cup *cold water;* stir into meat mixture. Cook and stir till thickened and bubbly. Season to taste. Serve over noodles. Makes 4 servings.

Meats

Beefy Tossed Salad
173/serving

  Creamy Salad Dressing
  (see recipe, page 75)
  6 ounces cooked lean beef, cut
  into thin bite-size strips
  4 cups torn iceberg lettuce
  3 cups torn romaine
  2 cups cauliflower flowerets
  1 cup cherry tomatoes, halved
  ½ cup shredded cheddar cheese
  ¼ cup sliced green onion

Prepare Creamy Salad Dressing; chill. Season beef with salt. In large salad bowl combine beef, iceberg lettuce, romaine, cauliflower, tomatoes, cheese, and green onion. Spoon dressing over all. Toss. Serves 4.

Yogurt Beefwiches
295/serving

  ½ pound lean ground beef
  ¼ cup chopped green pepper
  2 tablespoons chopped onion
  1 small clove garlic, minced
  1 teaspoon all-purpose flour
  ½ cup plain yogurt
  ½ teaspoon Worcestershire
  sauce
  2 individual French rolls
  1 medium tomato, sliced
  ½ cup shredded American
  cheese

Cook beef, pepper, onion, and garlic till meat is browned. Drain off fat. Stir flour into yogurt; stir yogurt mixture, Worcestershire, ½ teaspoon *salt*, and dash *pepper* into meat mixture. Heat through; *do not boil.*
  Slice rolls in half lengthwise. Place cut side up on baking sheet. Broil 4 to 5 inches from heat for 2 minutes or till toasted. Spread ¼ of the meat mixture atop each roll half. Place a tomato slice atop each. Place on baking sheet; broil 3 minutes. Sprinkle cheese atop; broil 2 minutes more. Serves 4.

Deluxe Beef Patties
306/serving

An herbed tomato sauce tops these broiled patties —

  1 beaten egg
  ¼ cup tomato juice
  2 tablespoons fine dry bread
  crumbs
  1 teaspoon Worcestershire
  sauce
  ½ teaspoon salt
  ½ teaspoon dried oregano,
  crushed
  ¼ teaspoon pepper
  Dash bottled hot pepper sauce
  1 pound lean ground beef
  ¼ cup chopped onion
  ¼ cup chopped green pepper
  1 clove garlic, minced
  2 teaspoons butter *or* margarine
  1 7½-ounce can tomatoes,
  cut up
  ¼ teaspoon dried oregano,
  crushed
  Dash bottled hot pepper sauce

Combine egg, tomato juice, bread crumbs, Worcestershire sauce, salt, ½ teaspoon oregano, pepper, and dash hot pepper sauce. Add meat; mix well. Shape into 4 patties, each ¾ inch thick. Broil patties 3 inches from heat for 6 minutes; season with salt and pepper. Turn patties; broil 6 minutes more for medium doneness.
  Meanwhile, prepare sauce. In small saucepan cook onion, green pepper, and garlic in butter or margarine till tender. Add *undrained* tomatoes, ¼ teaspoon oregano, and dash hot pepper sauce. Bring to boiling. Simmer, uncovered, 5 to 8 minutes or till sauce reaches desired consistency. Spoon over patties. Serves 4.

Spiced Pot Roast
186/serving

Caraway seed, peppercorns, cloves, and buttermilk make the flavor of this dish distinctive —

1	2½-pound beef chuck arm pot roast
2	tablespoons cooking oil
2	medium carrots, finely chopped
2	stalks celery, thinly sliced
1	medium onion, thinly sliced
1½	cups water
2	teaspoons instant beef bouillon granules
½	teaspoon caraway seed
5	whole black peppercorns
2	whole cloves
½	cup buttermilk
1	tablespoon cornstarch
¼	teaspoon Kitchen Bouquet (optional)

Trim excess fat from meat; sprinkle meat with salt and pepper. In Dutch oven brown meat on all sides in hot oil. Remove meat; add carrot, celery, and onion to Dutch oven. Cook vegetables till tender. Drain off excess fat. Return meat to Dutch oven. Add water, bouillon granules, and caraway seed. In double layer of cheesecloth tie together peppercorns and cloves; add to Dutch oven. Cover and simmer about 1½ hours or till meat is tender. Remove meat to warm serving platter. Discard cheesecloth bag. Skim excess fat from pan juices. In screw-top jar combine buttermilk and cornstarch; shake well. Add to drippings in Dutch oven. Cook and stir till thickened and bubbly. Add Kitchen Bouquet, if desired. Pour some gravy over meat; pass remainder. Makes 8 servings.

Serve fresh-tasting *Beefy Tossed Salad* or colorful *Ham and Cottage Cheese Mold* (see recipe, page 38) for a light meal.

33

Veal Stew—296/serving

- ¾ pound boneless lean veal, cut into ¾-inch cubes
- ¾ cup chopped onion
- 1 clove garlic, minced
- 2 tablespoons cooking oil
- 4 medium tomatoes, peeled, seeded, and chopped
- ¼ cup water
- 1 tablespoon paprika
- 1 teaspoon instant chicken bouillon granules
- Dash bottled hot pepper sauce
- 1 large green pepper, cut into thin strips
- 1⅓ cups hot cooked quick-cooking rice

In Dutch oven or large saucepan cook veal, onion, and garlic in hot oil till meat is browned and onion is tender. Drain off fat. Add tomatoes, water, paprika, bouillon granules, hot pepper sauce, and ¾ teaspoon *salt*. Cover and simmer for 30 minutes or till meat is tender, stirring occasionally. Add green pepper. Cover and simmer for 5 to 10 minutes more or till green pepper is tender. Serve over rice. Makes 4 servings.

Wine-Sauced Pot Roast 238/serving

- 1 3-pound beef chuck arm pot roast
- 1 tablespoon cooking oil
- ½ cup dry red wine
- 1 tablespoon instant beef bouillon granules
- ½ teaspoon dried rosemary, crushed
- ½ teaspoon dried basil, crushed
- ½ teaspoon pepper
- 16 large fresh mushrooms
- 4 large carrots, cut in julienne strips
- 8 small whole onions
- 4 tomatoes, quartered

Trim excess fat from meat. In Dutch oven brown meat on all sides in hot oil. Add wine, bouillon granules, rosemary, basil, and pepper. Cover and roast in 325° oven for 1 to 1¼ hours or till meat is nearly done. Add mushrooms, carrots, and onions to meat; spoon juices over vegetables. Cover and continue cooking for 40 minutes. Add tomatoes; cover and cook 5 to 10 minutes more or till vegetables and meat are tender. Remove meat and vegetables to a warm platter. Skim fat from juices and pass juices with meat and vegetables. Makes 8 servings.

Veal Chops with Lemon Sauce—219/serving

- 2 veal loin chops, cut ½ inch thick (½ pound)
- 1 2-ounce can sliced mushrooms
- 2 teaspoons butter *or* margarine
- ⅓ cup skim milk
- 1½ teaspoons cornstarch
- 2 teaspoons lemon juice
- ¼ teaspoon salt
- Dash dried tarragon, crushed
- Dash pepper

Place chops on unheated rack of broiler pan. Broil chops 3 to 4 inches from heat for 5 minutes. Turn chops; sprinkle with salt and pepper. Broil about 5 minutes more or till done. Meanwhile, in saucepan combine *undrained* mushrooms and butter. Cook over low heat till butter is melted. In screw-top jar combine milk and cornstarch; shake well. Add to mushrooms. Cook and stir over medium heat till thickened and bubbly. Remove from heat; stir in lemon juice, salt, tarragon, and pepper. Spoon sauce over chops. Makes 2 servings.

Barbecued Beef and Beans 250/serving

- ½ pound cooked lean beef, trimmed of separable fat
- ½ cup tomato sauce
- ¼ cup water
- 2 tablespoons finely chopped onion
- 2 tablespoons red wine vinegar
- 2 teaspoons brown sugar
- 2 teaspoons Worcestershire sauce
- 2 teaspoons prepared mustard
- 1 teaspoon paprika
- 1 teaspoon chili powder
- ¼ teaspoon salt
- 1 8-ounce can red kidney beans, drained
- 2 cups shredded lettuce
- ½ cup shredded cheddar cheese (2 ounces)

Cut cooked beef into thin strips; set aside. In saucepan combine tomato sauce, water, onion, red wine vinegar, brown sugar, Worcestershire sauce, mustard, paprika, chili powder, and salt. Bring to boiling; reduce heat. Simmer, covered, for 10 minutes, stirring occasionally. Stir in beef strips and kidney beans. Heat through. Serve atop shredded lettuce. Sprinkle shredded cheese atop each serving. Makes 4 servings.

Microwave directions: Cut beef into thin strips. In non-metal mixing bowl combine tomato sauce, water, onion, vinegar, brown sugar, Worcestershire, mustard, paprika, chili powder, and salt. Cover; cook in countertop microwave oven on high power for 6 minutes or till onion is tender. Add beef and kidney beans; microcook 2 minutes more or till heated through. Serve as above.

Steak-Tomato Stew
240/serving

    ¾ pound beef round steak,
        trimmed of separable fat
        and cubed
    1 clove garlic, minced
    1 tablespoon cooking oil
    3 medium carrots, sliced
        ½ inch thick (1½ cups)
    1 teaspoon instant beef
        bouillon granules
    ¼ teaspoon dried basil, crushed
    ¼ teaspoon dried thyme, crushed
    1 7½-ounce can tomatoes,
        cut up
    9 pearl onions or one 8-ounce
        can peeled small whole
        onions, drained
    ¼ cup chopped green pepper
    2 teaspoons cornstarch

In medium saucepan brown *half* the meat and the garlic in hot oil. Remove from saucepan; brown remaining meat. Return all meat to saucepan. Stir in carrots, bouillon granules, basil, thyme, and ¾ cup *water*. Simmer, covered, for 30 minutes. Stir in *undrained* tomatoes, onions, and green pepper. Simmer, covered, for 20 minutes more. Combine cornstarch and 1 tablespoon *cold water*; add to stew. Cook and stir till thickened and bubbly. Makes 3 servings.

Oriental Pork Chops
193/serving

    6 pork loin rib chops (2 pounds),
        cut ½ inch thick and
        trimmed of separable fat
    1 tablespoon cooking oil
    1 4-ounce can sliced mushrooms
    ½ cup water
    ½ cup sliced celery
    ¼ cup chopped onion
    1 tablespoon soy sauce
    1 teaspoon instant chicken
        bouillon granules
    2 teaspoons cornstarch
    8 water chestnuts, sliced

In large skillet brown chops in hot oil. Drain off fat. Add *undrained* mushrooms, ½ cup water, celery, onion, soy sauce, and bouillon granules. Cover and simmer for 40 minutes or till tender. Remove chops from skillet. Stir cornstarch into ¼ cup *cold water*; stir into mixture in skillet. Add water chestnuts. Cook and stir till mixture is thickened and bubbly. Cook and stir 1 to 2 minutes more. Pour some sauce over chops; pass remainder. Makes 6 servings.

Orange-Sauced Pork Chops
180/serving

    4 pork loin rib chops, cut
        ½ inch thick (1 to 1½
        pounds)
    1 tablespoon cooking oil
    1 tablespoon brown sugar
    ½ teaspoon finely shredded
        orange peel
    ¼ teaspoon salt
    ¼ teaspoon ground ginger
    ⅔ cup orange juice
    1 tablespoon cold water
    2 teaspoons cornstarch

Trim excess fat from chops. In skillet brown chops slowly in hot oil. Remove chops to 9x9x2-inch baking pan. Combine brown sugar, orange peel, salt, and ginger; stir in orange juice. Pour over chops. Cover and bake in 350° oven for 45 to 50 minutes or till chops are tender. Transfer chops to warm platter; keep warm. Skim fat from cooking liquid. Measure cooking liquid. If necessary, add water to cooking liquid to measure ¾ cup total. In saucepan combine cold water and cornstarch; add the ¾ cup liquid. Cook and stir till thickened and bubbly; cook and stir 2 minutes more. Spoon some sauce over chops; pass remainder. Makes 4 servings.

Festive Pork Roast
177/serving

    ½ cup dry red wine
    ¼ cup packed brown sugar
    3 tablespoons water
    3 tablespoons vinegar
    3 tablespoons catsup
    1 tablespoon cooking oil
    1 tablespoon soy sauce
    1 clove garlic, minced
    1 teaspoon curry powder
    ¼ teaspoon ground ginger
    ¼ teaspoon pepper
    1 5-pound boneless rolled pork
        loin roast
    ¼ cup cold water
    2 teaspoons cornstarch

For marinade, combine wine, brown sugar, 3 tablespoons water, vinegar, catsup, cooking oil, soy sauce, garlic, curry powder, ginger, and pepper. Trim fat from meat (see note). Place meat in plastic bag; set in shallow dish. Pour marinade into bag; close bag. Marinate meat in refrigerator for 6 to 8 hours or overnight, turning bag several times to distribute marinade. Drain meat, reserving 1 cup marinade. Pat meat dry with paper toweling. Place meat on rack in shallow roasting pan. Roast in 325° oven about 2 hours or till meat thermometer registers 160°.

Meanwhile, in small saucepan combine ¼ cup cold water and cornstarch; add reserved marinade. Cook and stir till thickened and bubbly. Cook and stir 1 to 2 minutes more. Brush roast with marinade mixture. Continue roasting about 1 hour or till meat thermometer registers 170°. Brush roast frequently with marinade mixture. Spoon remaining marinade mixture over meat before serving. Makes 20 servings.

Note: Untie the rolled roast to trim fat. Reroll roast into a compact shape; tie with kitchen string.

Main Dishes
Meats

Sauerkraut and Pork Skillet
220/serving

- 4 pork chops, cut ½ inch thick (about 1¼ pounds)
- 1 tablespoon cooking oil
- 1 medium onion, sliced and separated into rings
- 1 clove garlic, minced
- 1 16-ounce can sauerkraut, drained and snipped
- ½ cup apple juice *or* cider
- 1 teaspoon caraway seed
- ½ teaspoon salt
- ¼ teaspoon dried thyme, crushed
- ¼ teaspoon pepper
- 1 small apple, cored and sliced

In 10-inch skillet brown chops in hot oil; remove chops, reserving drippings in skillet. Cook onion and garlic in skillet drippings till onion is tender. Add sauerkraut, apple juice, caraway seed, ½ teaspoon salt, thyme, and pepper. Place chops atop; sprinkle with salt. Cover and simmer 20 minutes or till chops are tender. Add apple slices to skillet; cover and simmer 5 minutes or till apple is just tender. Makes 4 servings.

Pork Turnover—343/serving
pictured on pages 24 and 25

- ½ cup chopped green pepper
- ¼ cup chopped onion
- 1 tablespoon butter *or* margarine
- 1½ cups chopped cooked pork
- 1 8-ounce jar applesauce
- 2 tablespoons Dijon-style mustard
- ¾ teaspoon ground ginger
- 2 packages (6 biscuits each) refrigerated biscuits
  Milk (optional)
  Sesame seed (optional)

In a 2-quart saucepan cook green pepper and onion in butter or margarine till tender. Remove from heat; stir in pork, applesauce, mustard, ginger, and ½ teaspoon *salt*. On floured surface roll each biscuit to a 5-inch circle. Place ⅓ *cup* of the pork mixture on 6 of the dough rounds, spreading meat mixture to within ½ inch of edge. Top with remaining dough rounds. Press edges together; seal with tines of fork. Brush with milk and sprinkle with sesame seed, if desired. Place on an ungreased baking sheet. Bake in 400° oven for 10 to 12 minutes or till golden brown. Serve warm. Makes 6 servings.

Spicy Pork Skillet
283/serving
pictured on the cover, too

- ¾ pound boneless pork, cut into thin strips and trimmed of separable fat
- 1 medium onion, thinly sliced
- 1 tablespoon cooking oil
- 1 8-ounce can tomato sauce
- 1½ teaspoons chili powder
- 1 teaspoon Worcestershire sauce
- ¼ teaspoon cayenne
- 1 12-ounce can whole kernel corn, drained
- 1 large green pepper, cut into strips (1 cup)
- 1 2-ounce jar sliced pimiento, drained
- ¼ cup shredded cheddar cheese

In 10-inch skillet brown meat and onion in hot oil. Combine tomato sauce, chili powder, Worcestershire sauce, cayenne, ⅓ cup *water,* and ¼ teaspoon *salt*; add to meat. Cover and simmer for 15 minutes or till meat is tender. Stir in corn, green pepper, and pimiento. Simmer, uncovered, for 10 minutes or till green pepper is tender and some of the liquid has evaporated. Sprinkle cheese atop before serving. Serves 4.

Dilled Cabbage Rolls
244/serving
Cabbage leaves filled with a ground pork, mushroom, and yogurt mixture simmer in bouillon for flavor —

- 8 large cabbage leaves
- ½ pound ground pork
- ½ cup chopped fresh mushrooms
- ¼ cup chopped onion
- 1 cup cooked rice
- ½ cup plain yogurt
- 1 beaten egg
- ½ teaspoon dillweed
- ¼ teaspoon salt
- 2 teaspoons instant chicken bouillon granules
- 1 cup boiling water
- ¼ cup plain yogurt
  Snipped parsley

Cut about 2 inches of heavy center vein out of each cabbage leaf. Immerse leaves in boiling salted water about 3 minutes or just till limp; drain.

In 10-inch skillet cook ground pork, mushrooms, and onion till meat is browned and onion is tender. Remove from heat. Stir in cooked rice, ½ cup yogurt, egg, dillweed, and salt. Place about ¼ *cup* of the meat mixture in center of each leaf; fold in sides. Fold ends so they overlap atop meat mixture.

Place cabbage rolls, seam side down, in a 10-inch skillet. Dissolve bouillon granules in boiling water; pour over cabbage rolls. Cover and simmer about 25 minutes. Remove cabbage rolls with slotted spoon to serving platter. Top each cabbage roll with a dollop of yogurt and snipped parsley. Serve immediately. Makes 4 servings.

Lamb Zucchini Casserole (see recipe, page 41) and *Spicy Pork Skillet* are easy-on-the-cook dishes.

Main Dishes
Meats

Ham and Cheese Casserole
293/serving

Ham, peas, carrots, and mushrooms in a cheesy sauce —

- 1 cup sliced fresh mushrooms
- ½ cup chopped onion
- ¼ cup chopped green pepper
- 2 tablespoons butter *or* margarine
- 1⅓ cups *reconstituted* nonfat dry milk
- 4 teaspoons cornstarch
- ¼ teaspoon dry mustard
- ¼ teaspoon pepper
- ¾ cup shredded *process* Swiss cheese
- 1¼ cups chopped fully cooked ham
- 1 10-ounce package frozen peas and carrots, thawed

In 2-quart saucepan cook mushrooms, chopped onion, and green pepper in butter or margarine till vegetables are tender but not brown. In screw-top jar combine reconstituted milk, cornstarch, dry mustard, and pepper; shake well to mix. Stir into mushroom mixture. Cook, stirring constantly, over medium heat till mixture is thickened and bubbly. Stir in ½ *cup* of the shredded Swiss cheese and stir to melt the cheese. Stir in the chopped ham and the peas and carrots. Transfer ham-vegetable mixture to a 1½-quart casserole. Cover and bake in a 350° oven for 30 minutes or till heated through. Sprinkle remaining shredded Swiss cheese atop. Bake 5 minutes more or till cheese is melted. Makes 4 servings.

Ham and Cottage Cheese Mold—128/serving

pictured on page 33

- 1 envelope unflavored gelatin
- 1 cup cold water
- 1 teaspoon instant chicken bouillon granules
- 1 cup plain yogurt
- 1 cup ground fully cooked ham
- ½ cup finely chopped celery
- ½ cup cream-style cottage cheese
- 2 tablespoons chopped pimiento
- 2 tablespoons chopped green pepper
- 1 tablespoon sliced green onion
- Lettuce
- Shredded carrot (optional)

Soften gelatin in cold water; add bouillon granules. Heat, stirring constantly, till gelatin and bouillon granules dissolve. Remove from heat. Add yogurt; beat with rotary beater till smooth. Chill mixture till partially set (consistency of unbeaten egg whites). Fold in ham, celery, cottage cheese, pimiento, green pepper, and onion. Pour into 4 individual molds. Chill till firm. Unmold onto individual lettuce-lined plates. Garnish with shredded carrot, if desired. Makes 4 servings.

Orange-Ginger Ham Grill
332/serving

- 2 tablespoons dry white wine
- 2 tablespoons frozen orange juice concentrate, thawed
- ½ teaspoon dry mustard
- ⅛ teaspoon ground ginger
- 1 1½-pound fully cooked ham slice, cut 1 inch thick and trimmed of separable fat
- 6 canned pineapple slices

Combine wine, orange juice concentrate, dry mustard, and ginger. Slash edge of ham slice. Brush sauce over ham. Grill over *medium* coals for 10 to 15 minutes, brushing with sauce occasionally. Turn ham, and grill 10 to 15 minutes more or till done, brushing with sauce. Grill pineapple slices alongside the ham during the last 5 to 10 minutes of grilling. Serves 6.

Apple Ham Slice
252/serving

- 2 tablespoons butter *or* margarine
- 1 2-pound fully cooked ham slice, cut 1 inch thick and trimmed of separable fat
- ¼ cup sliced green onion
- ¾ cup apple juice *or* apple cider
- ½ teaspoon ground cinnamon
- 1 tablespoon cornstarch
- 1 tablespoon cold water
- 2 medium apples
- ¼ cup raisins

In large skillet melt butter. Brown ham on both sides in butter; remove from skillet. Cook onion in butter till tender. Stir in apple juice and cinnamon; bring to boiling. Combine cornstarch and water; stir into apple juice mixture. Cook and stir till thickened and bubbly. Return ham to skillet. Cover; simmer for 10 minutes. Peel, core, and slice apples. Place apple slices atop ham and add raisins to skillet. Cook, covered, 5 to 7 minutes more or till apples are just tender. Transfer ham to warm platter; spoon some sauce and fruit atop. Pass remaining sauce. Makes 6 servings.

Yogurt-Sauced Pork Balls
264/serving

The sauce is so rich tasting, it's like sour cream —

- 1 beaten egg
- ⅓ cup fine dry bread crumbs
- 3 tablespoons plain yogurt
- 4 teaspoons finely chopped onion
- ½ teaspoon salt
- ¼ teaspoon pepper
- 1 pound ground pork
- 1 tablespoon cooking oil
- 1½ teaspoons instant beef bouillon granules
- 1 cup boiling water
- 2 tablespoons catsup
- 1 teaspoon Worcestershire sauce
- ½ teaspoon dried basil, crushed
- 3 tablespoons cold water
- 1 tablespoon cornstarch
- ⅓ cup plain yogurt

In bowl combine egg, the bread crumbs, 3 tablespoons yogurt, onion, salt, and pepper. Add ground pork; mix well. Shape into 32 meatballs. In skillet brown meatballs in hot oil. Drain off fat. Dissolve bouillon granules in boiling water; add catsup, Worcestershire sauce, and basil. Add to skillet. Bring to boiling. Reduce heat; cover and simmer 20 minutes. Remove meatballs to serving dish. Skim fat from pan juices. Measure pan juices. Add water, if necessary, to measure ¾ cup liquid. Return to skillet. Stir cold water into cornstarch; add to liquid in skillet. Cook and stir till thickened and bubbly. Stir in ⅓ cup plain yogurt. Heat through but *do not boil*. Serve immediately. Makes 4 servings.

Broil Pork Chops for Low-Calorie Eating

Broiling is an excellent calorie cutting cooking technique because it adds no extra butter, margarine, or oil. Fats naturally present in foods remain in the broiler pan, while the natural flavor and juices stay inside the food.

Many foods, including such favorites as beef steaks and fish fillets, are good for broiling. Pork chops also are excellent for broiling because of their lean meat; after being broiled the chops are tender and juicy.

To broil pork chops, choose pork rib or loin chops that are ¾ to 1 inch thick. Set the oven temperature to "broil" and preheat if desired (check range instruction booklet). Place chops on unheated rack of broiler pan (food will stick to a hot broiler rack). Place chops 3 to 4 inches from heat. (To position the rack, measure the distance from the top of the pork chops to the heat source.) Season chops with salt and pepper. Broil for 10 to 13 minutes, then turn using tongs. Continue broiling chops for 10 to 12 minutes more or till done.

Before serving, trim away excess fat. One 5-ounce raw pork loin chop (with bone) that has been broiled has 151 calories. If desired, serve broiled pork chops with a low-calorie sauce.

Spicy Ham Patties with Apple Rings—275/serving

- 2 beaten eggs
- ½ cup applesauce
- 1½ cups soft bread crumbs (2 slices)
- ⅓ cup nonfat dry milk powder
- ¼ cup chopped onion
- ½ teaspoon dry mustard
- ¼ teaspoon salt
- ¾ pound ground fully cooked ham
- ½ pound ground pork
- 1 tablespoon brown sugar
- 2 teaspoons cornstarch
- ¼ teaspoon dry mustard
  Dash ground cloves
- ¾ cup applesauce
- 1 tablespoon vinegar
- 1 medium apple, cored and sliced into 6 rings
  Snipped parsley (optional)

In mixing bowl combine beaten eggs, the ½ cup applesauce, and the bread crumbs; stir in nonfat dry milk powder, chopped onion, ½ teaspoon dry mustard, and the salt. Add ground ham and ground pork; mix well. Shape meat mixture into 6 patties; place in 13x9x2-inch baking pan. Bake in 350° oven for 40 to 45 minutes or till done.

Meanwhile, prepare sauce. In saucepan combine brown sugar, cornstarch, ¼ teaspoon dry mustard, and the cloves. Stir in the ¾ cup applesauce and the vinegar. Cook and stir till thickened and bubbly. Add apple rings; cover and simmer about 15 minutes or till apple rings are just tender. To serve, arrange an apple ring atop each patty. Spoon sauce over. Garnish with parsley, if desired. Makes 6 servings.

Main Dishes
Meats

Cooking with Yogurt

Yogurt is used often in this book because it is low in calories yet adds a delightful flavor to foods. Try substituting yogurt for mayonnaise or sour cream to cut calories in your favorite recipes. A tablespoon of low-fat plain yogurt has only 8 calories compared with 101 for mayonnaise and 26 for sour cream. When using yogurt in a sauce, stir it in at the end of cooking; heat through but do not boil. Also when adding it to a hot or cold mixture, blend yogurt gently. Vigorous stirring causes it to thin.

Ham with Pineapple Sauce
165/serving

- 1 2-pound fully cooked boneless ham
- 1 8-ounce can crushed pineapple (juice pack)
- 1 teaspoon cornstarch
- ½ teaspoon finely shredded orange peel
- ¼ teaspoon ground cinnamon
    Dash ground cloves
- 1 large orange
- 2 teaspoons butter *or* margarine

Place ham on rack in shallow baking pan. Insert meat thermometer. Bake in 325° oven for 1 hour or till meat thermometer registers 140°.

Meanwhile, in saucepan combine *undrained* pineapple, cornstarch, orange peel, cinnamon, and cloves. Peel and section orange, reserving juice. Chop orange sections; add sections and reserved juice to pineapple mixture. Cook and stir till thickened and bubbly. Stir in butter till melted. To serve, slice ham; spoon sauce over. Makes 8 servings.

Glazed Ham Kebabs
209/serving

- 2 medium sweet potatoes (about 10 ounces)
- ¾ pound fully cooked boneless ham, trimmed of separable fat
- 2 small onions, cut in wedges
- ¼ cup orange juice
- 1 tablespoon light molasses
- 1 tablespoon vinegar
- 1 teaspoon cornstarch

Cut off woody portion of sweet potatoes. In saucepan cook potatoes, covered, in enough boiling salted water to cover for 25 minutes or till tender. Drain; cool. Peel and cut into 1-inch pieces. Cut ham into 1-inch cubes. On four skewers, alternately thread ham pieces, sweet potato pieces, and onion wedges.

For glaze, in saucepan combine orange juice, molasses, vinegar, and cornstarch. Cook and stir till thickened and bubbly. Brush glaze over kebabs. Grill over *medium* coals about 15 minutes, brushing occasionally with glaze. Makes 4 servings.

Ham Stew—159/serving

- 1 16-ounce can tomatoes, cut up
- 1 16-ounce can mixed vegetables
- 1 cup diced fully cooked ham
- ¼ cup water
- 1 tablespoon snipped parsley
- ½ teaspoon dried thyme, crushed
- ½ teaspoon instant chicken bouillon granules
    Dash pepper
    Dash bottled hot pepper sauce

Combine *undrained* tomatoes, *undrained* mixed vegetables, ham, water, parsley, thyme, chicken bouillon granules, pepper, and hot pepper sauce. Bring to boiling; reduce heat. Cover and simmer about 10 minutes, stirring occasionally. Serves 4.

Belgian Lamb Stew
242/serving

Turnips, endive, herbs, and spices give this easy stew its unique flavor —

- 2 tablespoons cooking oil
- 2 pounds boneless lamb, cut into 1-inch cubes
- 2 cloves garlic, minced
- 1 large onion, chopped
- 1½ cups water
- 1 10½-ounce can condensed beef broth
- 1 teaspoon salt
- 1 bay leaf
- ½ teaspoon dried thyme, crushed
- ⅛ teaspoon ground cloves
- ⅛ teaspoon pepper
- 8 tiny new potatoes
- 4 small turnips, quartered
- 3 bunches Belgian endive
- 3 tablespoons cornstarch
- ¼ cup snipped parsley

In 4½-quart Dutch oven heat cooking oil over medium heat. Add *half* of the lamb, turning to brown on all sides. Remove lamb; set aside. Cook remaining lamb and garlic till browned. Add first half of lamb and onion; cook till onion is tender. Add water, beef broth, salt, bay leaf, thyme, cloves, and pepper. Bring to boiling; simmer, covered, 40 minutes. Add unpeeled potatoes and turnips; simmer, covered, 30 minutes more.

Trim off base of each bunch of endive; slice into ½-inch lengths. Place endive atop stew; simmer 5 to 8 minutes. Stir cornstarch into 3 tablespoons *cold water*. Add to stew. Bring to boiling over medium heat, stirring constantly; boil 1 minute. Stir in the snipped parsley. Serve in soup bowls. Makes 8 servings.

Curried Yogurt Kebabs
215/serving

- 1 8-ounce carton plain yogurt
- ¼ cup finely chopped green onion
- 3 tablespoons skim milk
- 1 teaspoon curry powder
- ½ teaspoon salt
- ½ teaspoon Worcestershire sauce
- 1½ pounds boneless leg of lamb, cut in 1-inch cubes
- 6 large fresh mushrooms
- 6 small boiled potatoes
- 6 cherry tomatoes

In small bowl combine yogurt, onion, milk, curry powder, salt, and Worcestershire sauce. Set aside. Thread meat alternately with mushrooms and potatoes on 6 skewers. Brush yogurt mixture on kebabs. Broil kebabs about 4 inches from heat for 10 to 12 minutes, brushing with yogurt mixture and giving a quarter turn every 3 minutes. Add a cherry tomato to the end of each skewer before serving. Makes 6 servings.

Marinated Lamb Kebabs
137/serving
Use a salad dressing with no more than 25 calories per tablespoon—

- ¾ pound boneless lean lamb, trimmed of separable fat
- ½ cup low-calorie Italian salad dressing
- 2 tablespoons lemon juice
- 8 fresh large mushrooms
- ¼ teaspoon Kitchen Bouquet (optional)
- 4 small zucchini, cut into 1-inch pieces

Cut meat into 1-inch pieces. Place meat in plastic bag; add salad dressing and lemon juice. Close bag and place in a bowl. Refrigerate several hours or overnight, turning bag occasionally to distribute marinade. Drain meat, reserve marinade. Add Kitchen Bouquet to marinade, if desired.

In bowl pour boiling water on mushrooms; drain immediately. Thread meat on skewers alternately with mushrooms and zucchini. Place on unheated rack of broiler pan. Broil 4 inches from heat for 10 to 12 minutes; turn and baste with marinade occasionally. Makes 4 servings.

Mint-Glazed Lamb Chops
109/serving

- ¼ cup cold water
- 1 teaspoon cornstarch
- 3 tablespoons finely snipped fresh mint leaves or 4 teaspoons dried mint flakes, crushed
- 1 tablespoon light corn syrup
- ½ teaspoon finely shredded lemon peel
- ¼ teaspoon salt
- 4 lamb leg sirloin chops, cut ¾ inch thick (about 1¼ pounds)

For glaze, in saucepan combine water and cornstarch. Add mint, corn syrup, lemon peel, and salt. Cook and stir till thickened and bubbly.

Place lamb chops on unheated rack of broiler pan. Broil 3 to 4 inches from heat for 5 minutes. Brush some glaze over chops. Turn chops; broil 5 to 6 minutes more, brushing occasionally with glaze. Makes 4 servings.

Lamb Zucchini Casserole
176/serving
pictured on page 37

- 1 pound boneless lean lamb, cut into thin bite-size strips and trimmed of separable fat
- ¾ cup chopped onion
- 1 clove garlic, minced
- 1 tablespoon cooking oil
- 2 10-ounce packages frozen chopped spinach, thawed and well drained (see note)
- ½ teaspoon dried basil, crushed Dash ground nutmeg
- 1½ cups shredded mozzarella cheese (6 ounces)
- ½ teaspoon salt
- ⅔ cup cold water
- 1 teaspoon instant chicken bouillon granules
- 1 teaspoon cornstarch
- 2 small zucchini, thinly sliced
- ¼ cup grated Parmesan cheese
- ¼ teaspoon dried basil, crushed

In skillet brown the meat, onion, and garlic in hot oil. Drain off the fat. In large bowl combine spinach, ½ teaspoon basil, and nutmeg; stir in drained meat mixture, mozzarella cheese, and salt. Combine water, bouillon granules, and cornstarch; add to spinach mixture. Mix well; turn mixture into a 10x6x2-inch baking dish or other oblong baking dish. Arrange zucchini slices atop, overlapping as necessary. Sprinkle with Parmesan cheese and ¼ teaspoon basil. Bake, covered, in a 350° oven for 30 minutes or till zucchini is crisp-tender. Uncover and bake 5 to 10 minutes more or till golden. Serves 8.

Note: Press out any excess liquid in the spinach.

Main Dishes
Meats

Creamy Lamb Crepes
275/serving

Neufchâtel cheese adds a special richness to the filling —

8 Calorie Counter's Crepes
   (see recipe, page 20)
½ pound boneless lean lamb,
   cut into thin strips
1 tablespoon all-purpose flour
¼ teaspoon salt
   Dash pepper
¼ cup chopped onion
1 tablespoon butter or
   margarine
¼ cup water
3 tablespoons dry sherry
⅛ teaspoon dried marjoram,
   crushed
   Dash ground nutmeg
3 ounces Neufchâtel
   cheese, cubed
2 tablespoons skim milk
¼ cup shredded Swiss cheese
   (1 ounce)

Prepare Calorie Counter's Crepes. Trim excess fat from meat. Coat meat strips in a mixture of the flour, salt, and pepper. In skillet brown meat strips and onion in butter or margarine. Stir in water, sherry, marjoram, and nutmeg. Simmer, covered, 15 to 20 minutes or till lamb is tender. Stir in Neufchâtel cheese and skim milk. Spoon meat filling along center of unbrowned side of each crepe; fold two opposite edges so they overlap atop filling. Place crepes, seam side down, into a 12x7½x2-inch baking dish. Bake, covered, in 350° oven 10 minutes. Sprinkle with Swiss cheese. Bake, uncovered, 5 minutes more or till cheese is melted. If desired, sprinkle with snipped parsley. Makes 4 servings.

Orange-Sauced Lamb Chops
134/serving

1 tablespoon cornstarch
¼ teaspoon finely shredded
   orange peel
⅛ teaspoon ground nutmeg
¾ cup orange juice
1 teaspoon lemon juice
4 lamb loin chops, cut ¾ inch
   thick
½ cup seedless green grapes,
   halved

In saucepan combine cornstarch, orange peel, and nutmeg; stir in orange juice. Cook and stir till thickened and bubbly. Stir in lemon juice. Brush chops with sauce. Broil chops 3 to 4 inches from heat for 4 minutes; turn and brush with sauce again. Broil chops 5 to 6 minutes longer. Stir grapes into remaining sauce; heat through. Spoon sauce atop chops. Makes 4 servings.

Herbed Lamb Stew
249/serving

1 pound boneless lean lamb,
   trimmed of separable fat
½ cup chopped onion
1 tablespoon cooking oil
1 cup water
¼ cup dry white wine
1½ teaspoons instant chicken
   bouillon granules
½ teaspoon dried basil, crushed
½ teaspoon dried thyme, crushed
¼ teaspoon dry mustard
2 carrots, cut into 1-inch
   pieces
2 potatoes, peeled and cubed
2 stalks celery, sliced into
   1-inch pieces
1 cup fresh green beans
1 green pepper, cut into
   1-inch pieces
1 tablespoon cornstarch
2 tablespoons cold water

In Dutch oven brown the meat and onion in hot oil. Drain off fat. Add water, wine, bouillon granules, basil, thyme, and dry mustard. Bring to boiling. Reduce heat; cover and simmer about 30 minutes or till meat is tender. Add carrots, potatoes, celery, beans, and green pepper. Cover and simmer for 20 to 25 minutes or till vegetables are tender. Combine cornstarch and water; stir into stew. Cook and stir till thickened and bubbly. Cook and stir 1 to 2 minutes more. Makes 4 servings.

Onion Braised Lamb Chops
228/serving

4 lamb loin chops, cut 1 inch
   thick and trimmed of
   separable fat
1 tablespoon cooking oil
1 small onion, sliced
½ cup water
½ teaspoon instant chicken
   bouillon granules
⅛ teaspoon dried thyme, crushed
2 tablespoons skim milk
1 teaspoon cornstarch
2 tablespoons plain yogurt

In skillet brown chops on both sides in hot oil. Drain off excess fat. Add onion, water, bouillon granules, and thyme. Cover and simmer for 15 to 20 minutes or till meat is tender. Remove meat to platter; keep warm. Skim excess fat from skillet juices. Stir milk into cornstarch; add to skillet. Cook and stir over medium heat till mixture is thickened and bubbly. Stir in yogurt; heat through (do not boil). Spoon sauce over chops. Makes 2 servings.

Poultry

Plum-Sauced Chicken
236/serving

Soy sauce and ginger add Oriental spice to this dish —

- 1 2½- to 3-pound broiler-fryer chicken, cut up
- ½ teaspoon salt
- ¼ teaspoon pepper
- ⅓ cup plum preserves
- ¼ cup finely chopped onion
- 2 tablespoons frozen orange juice concentrate, thawed
- 1 tablespoon soy sauce
- 1 teaspoon prepared mustard
- ½ teaspoon ground ginger
- ¼ cup dry white wine
- 1 tablespoon cornstarch
- 1 tablespoon cold water
- ½ teaspoon instant chicken bouillon granules
  Few drops Kitchen Bouquet (optional)

Remove skin from chicken pieces; season with the salt and pepper. In large skillet combine preserves, onion, orange juice concentrate, soy sauce, mustard, and ginger. Simmer, uncovered, for 10 minutes. Stir in wine. Add chicken pieces; spoon plum mixture over chicken. Cover and simmer for 40 to 45 minutes or till chicken is tender; baste occasionally with plum mixture. Remove chicken to warm serving platter; keep warm.

Skim excess fat from pan juices. Measure 1 cup juices; return to skillet. Stir together cornstarch, cold water, and bouillon granules; add to pan juices. Cook and stir till thickened and bubbly. Stir in Kitchen Bouquet, if desired. Spoon some sauce atop chicken. Pass remaining sauce. Makes 6 servings.

Chicken Veronique
218/serving

Chicken breasts in a wine-grape sauce —

- 2 whole medium chicken breasts, skinned, boned, and halved lengthwise
- ½ small lemon
- 1 tablespoon butter or margarine
- ⅓ cup dry white wine
- 2 tablespoons water
- ¼ teaspoon instant chicken bouillon granules
  Paprika
- 1 tablespoon cold water
- 2 teaspoons cornstarch
- ¾ cup seedless green grapes, halved
  Lemon slices (optional)

Rub chicken well with the lemon; sprinkle lightly with salt. In skillet brown chicken slowly in hot butter or margarine about 10 minutes, turning chicken pieces as necessary to brown evenly. Drain off fat. Add wine, 2 tablespoons water, and the chicken bouillon granules. Cover and simmer for 25 to 35 minutes or till chicken is tender, spooning wine mixture over chicken occasionally. Remove chicken to serving platter. Sprinkle with paprika; keep warm. Skim fat from pan juices. Measure juices, adding water if necessary to make ¾ cup. Return juices to pan. Stir 1 tablespoon cold water into cornstarch; stir into juices. Cook and stir over medium heat till mixture is thickened and bubbly. Add grapes and heat through. Spoon over chicken. Garnish with lemon slices, if desired. Makes 4 servings.

Low-Calorie Cooking Tips for Poultry

When preparing poultry remove its skin to reduce calories. This will remove about 20 calories per serving.

Also, try to prepare poultry recipes using light meat (breasts) rather than dark meat (thighs and legs). One cup of chopped cooked light meat (without skin) has 232 calories; a cup of chopped cooked dark meat (without skin) has 246 calories.

Tomato-Broccoli Chicken
244/serving

- 2 whole medium chicken breasts, skinned, boned, and halved lengthwise
- ¼ cup chopped onion
- 2 tablespoons butter or margarine
- 1 10-ounce package frozen cut broccoli, thawed
- 1 teaspoon lemon juice
- ¼ teaspoon dried thyme, crushed
- 3 medium tomatoes, cut into wedges

Sprinkle chicken lightly with a little salt and pepper. Cut chicken into ½-inch-wide strips. In medium skillet cook chicken and onion in butter or margarine till chicken no longer is pink. Stir in broccoli, lemon juice, thyme, ¾ teaspoon *salt,* and ⅛ teaspoon *pepper.* Cover; simmer 6 minutes. Add tomatoes. Simmer, covered, 3 to 4 minutes more. Makes 4 servings.

Main Dishes
Poultry

Three-Cheese Chicken Bake
318/serving

Layers of pasta, cheeses, and chicken make this dish similar to a traditional baked lasagne. A real treat for calorie watchers —

- 8 ounces lasagne noodles
- ½ cup chopped onion
- ½ cup chopped green pepper
- 3 tablespoons butter *or* margarine
- 1 10¾-ounce can condensed cream of chicken soup
- 1 4-ounce can sliced mushrooms, drained
- ½ cup chopped pimiento
- ⅓ cup skim milk
- ½ teaspoon dried basil, crushed
- 1½ cups cream-style cottage cheese
- 2 cups chopped cooked chicken *or* turkey
- 1½ cups shredded American cheese
- ½ cup grated Parmesan cheese

Cook lasagne noodles in boiling salted water according to package directions; drain well. Cook onion and green pepper in butter or margarine till tender. Stir in condensed soup, mushrooms, pimiento, skim milk, and basil.

Lay *half* the noodles in a 13x9x2-inch baking dish; top with *half* each of the soup mixture, cottage cheese, chicken, American cheese, and Parmesan cheese. Repeat layers of the noodles, sauce, cottage cheese, and chicken.

Bake in 350° oven for 45 minutes. Top with remaining American and Parmesan cheese; bake 2 minutes more or till cheese is melted. Makes 10 servings.

Quick Chicken Vegetable Soup—155/serving

- 1 7½-ounce can tomatoes, cut up
- 1 cup sliced carrot
- ½ cup chopped onion
- ¼ cup chopped green pepper
- 1½ teaspoons instant chicken bouillon granules
- ½ teaspoon dried thyme, crushed
- ¼ teaspoon ground sage
- ⅛ teaspoon pepper
- ¾ cup chopped cooked chicken

In saucepan combine *undrained* tomatoes, carrot, onion, green pepper, bouillon granules, thyme, sage, pepper, and 1 cup *water*. Bring to boiling. Cover; simmer for 15 minutes or till vegetables are tender. Stir in chicken; heat through. Serves 2.

Wine-Sauced Chicken Livers
179/serving

- 1 medium onion, sliced and separated into rings
- ½ cup green pepper strips
- 1 tablespoon butter *or* margarine
- 1 pound chicken livers, halved
- 1 cup skim milk
- 4 teaspoons cornstarch
- ½ teaspoon salt
- 1 4-ounce can sliced mushrooms, drained
- 2 tablespoons snipped parsley
- 2 tablespoons dry white wine

In covered skillet cook onion and green pepper in butter or margarine till tender but not brown. Add chicken livers; cook, uncovered, 4 to 5 minutes or till livers are just barely pink inside. Combine milk, cornstarch, salt, and ¼ teaspoon *pepper*; add to liver mixture. Cook and stir till thickened and bubbly. Add mushrooms, parsley, and wine; heat through. Makes 6 servings.

Elegant Chicken Crepes
278/serving

pictured on the cover, too

- 12 Calorie Counter's Crepes (see recipe, page 20)
- ¼ cup chopped onion
- ¼ cup water
- 1 cup skim milk
- 2 tablespoons cornstarch
- ¼ teaspoon salt
- ⅛ teaspoon pepper
- 1 cup shredded *process* Swiss cheese (4 ounces)
- 1 4-ounce can sliced mushrooms, drained
- 2 cups finely chopped cooked chicken
- 1 10-ounce package frozen chopped broccoli, cooked and drained

Prepare Calorie Counter's Crepes; set aside. In saucepan combine onion and water. Cook, covered, 5 minutes. *Do not drain.* Combine milk, cornstarch, salt, and pepper; add to onion. Cook and stir till thickened and bubbly. Cook and stir 1 minute more. Add cheese; stir to melt. Reserve ½ *cup* of the cheese mixture. Add mushrooms to remaining cheese mixture. Cover; set aside.

For filling, combine chicken, broccoli, and the ½ cup reserved cheese mixture. Spoon about ¼ *cup* filling on the unbrowned side of each crepe; roll up. Arrange crepes in a 13x9x2-inch baking dish. Cover and bake in 350° oven for 20 minutes. Meanwhile, heat cheese-mushroom mixture; serve over crepes. Serves 6.

Elegant Chicken Crepes are topped with a mushroom-cheese sauce before serving. ▷

Spicy Turkey Drumsticks
259/serving

- 2 fresh *or* frozen turkey legs (2 to 2½ pounds total)
- 1 7½-ounce can tomatoes, cut up
- ½ cup chopped onion
- 2 tablespoons chopped canned green chili peppers
- 2 tablespoons chopped pimiento
- 1 clove garlic, minced
- ¼ teaspoon Kitchen Bouquet
- ⅛ teaspoon cayenne
- 2 tablespoons cold water
- 2 teaspoons cornstarch

Remove skin from turkey legs. Place turkey legs in an 11x7x1½-inch baking pan. Season with salt and pepper. In small saucepan combine tomatoes, onion, chili peppers, pimiento, garlic, Kitchen Bouquet, and cayenne. Bring to boiling; reduce heat and simmer 3 to 4 minutes or till onion is tender. Pour sauce over turkey legs. Bake, covered, in 375° oven for 1 to 1½ hours or till turkey is tender. Remove turkey legs to serving platter; keep warm. Skim fat from pan juices. Transfer juices to small saucepan. Combine cold water and cornstarch; stir into juices. Cook and stir till thickened and bubbly. Spoon some sauce over turkey legs; pass remainder. Makes 4 servings.

Chicken and Pea Pods
247/serving

- 1 whole medium chicken breast, skinned, boned, and halved lengthwise
- 3 tablespoons water
- 3 tablespoons soy sauce
- ½ teaspoon grated gingerroot
- 1 6-ounce package frozen pea pods
- 2 tablespoons sliced green onion
- 1 teaspoon butter *or* margarine

Place each chicken breast half between two pieces of clear plastic wrap. Pound with flat side of meat mallet to ¼-inch thickness. Remove plastic; place chicken in shallow dish. Combine water, soy sauce, and gingerroot; pour over chicken. Cover and marinate in refrigerator for 1 hour. Drain chicken; reserve marinade. Broil chicken 3 to 4 inches from heat for 2 to 3 minutes per side, brushing with reserved marinade occasionally. Cook pea pods and onion in boiling salted water according to directions on package. Toss cooked vegetables with the butter or margarine; turn onto a platter. Top with chicken pieces. Garnish with lemon slices, if desired. Makes 2 servings.

Turkey Loaf—184/serving

- 1 beaten egg
- 1 2-ounce can mushroom stems and pieces, drained and chopped
- ½ cup shredded carrot
- ¼ cup orange juice
- ¼ cup fine dry bread crumbs
- 2 tablespoons snipped parsley
- ¾ teaspoon salt
- ¼ teaspoon poultry seasoning Dash pepper
- 1 pound ground raw turkey

In bowl combine egg, mushrooms, carrot, orange juice, bread crumbs, parsley, salt, poultry seasoning, and pepper. Add ground raw turkey; mix well. Press evenly into a 9-inch pie plate. Bake in 350° oven about 35 minutes or till done. Drain off any excess fat. Let stand 10 minutes; loosen edges and transfer to serving platter. Sprinkle with additional snipped parsley, if desired. Makes 6 servings.

Curry-Sauced Chicken
171/serving

- ¾ cup water
- ½ cup chopped apple
- 2 tablespoons sliced green onion
- 1 teaspoon instant chicken bouillon granules
- 1 teaspoon curry powder
- 1 small clove garlic, minced Dash pepper
- 2 whole medium chicken breasts, skinned and halved lengthwise
- 1 4-ounce can sliced mushrooms
- 1 tablespoon cornstarch

In 10-inch skillet combine water, apple, green onion, bouillon granules, curry powder, garlic, and pepper; bring to boiling. Add chicken; reduce heat. Cover and simmer for 25 to 30 minutes or till chicken is tender. Remove chicken to warm platter. Drain mushrooms, reserving ⅓ cup liquid. Combine ⅓ cup mushroom liquid and cornstarch; stir into pan juices. Cook and stir over medium heat till bubbly. Stir in the mushrooms. Spoon sauce over chicken. Makes 4 servings.

Microwave directions: In 2-quart nonmetal casserole combine water, apple, green onion, bouillon granules, curry powder, garlic, and pepper. Cook in countertop microwave oven on high power for 2 minutes. Add chicken pieces; micro-cook, covered, 12 to 15 minutes or till chicken is tender, rearranging chicken after 8 minutes. Remove chicken to platter. Drain mushrooms, reserving ⅓ cup liquid. Combine reserved mushroom liquid and cornstarch; stir into juices with mushrooms. Micro-cook for 3 minutes or till thickened and bubbly, stirring after each minute. Spoon sauce over chicken.

Sauced Chicken over Rusks
236/serving

- 1 cup sliced fresh mushrooms
- ½ cup chopped onion
- ½ cup chopped celery
- 1½ cups skim milk
- 4 teaspoons cornstarch
- 1 teaspoon instant chicken bouillon granules
- ¼ teaspoon salt
- ⅛ teaspoon dried thyme, crushed
  Dash pepper
- ½ pound cooked chicken, cut in strips
- 2 tablespoons snipped parsley
- 2 tablespoons dry white wine
- 8 rusks

In saucepan cook mushrooms, onion, and celery in small amount of boiling water till onion is tender; drain. Combine milk, cornstarch, bouillon granules, salt, thyme, and pepper. Add to vegetables in saucepan. Cook and stir till thickened and bubbly. Stir in the chicken, parsley, and wine. Heat through. To serve, spoon chicken mixture over rusks. Makes 4 servings.

Fruited Barbecue Chicken
237/serving

- 1 8-ounce can tomato sauce
- 2 tablespoons vinegar
- 2 tablespoons brown sugar
- 2 teaspoons cooking oil
- 1 teaspoon minced dried onion
- 1 teaspoon Worcestershire sauce
- ¾ teaspoon paprika
  Dash garlic powder
- 1 8-ounce can crushed pineapple (juice pack), drained
- 1 2½- to 3-pound broiler-fryer chicken, cut up and skinned
- 2 teaspoons cornstarch
- 1 11-ounce can mandarin orange sections, drained

In skillet combine tomato sauce, vinegar, brown sugar, cooking oil, minced dried onion, Worcestershire sauce, paprika, garlic powder, and dash *pepper*. Bring to boiling. Stir in pineapple. Add chicken pieces. Cover; simmer about 40 minutes or till chicken is tender, basting with sauce occasionally. Remove chicken to platter; keep warm. Skim fat from sauce in skillet. Combine cornstarch and 1 tablespoon cold *water*; add to sauce. Cook and stir till bubbly. Stir in mandarin orange sections; heat through. Spoon sauce over chicken. Makes 6 servings.

Herbed Tomato Chicken
185/serving

- 2 medium onions, sliced
- 2 cloves garlic, minced
- ½ cup water
- 3 whole medium chicken breasts, skinned and halved lengthwise
- 1 7½-ounce can tomatoes, cut up
- ½ cup tomato sauce
- 1 2½-ounce jar sliced mushrooms, drained
- ¼ cup chopped green pepper
- 1 teaspoon dried basil, crushed
- 1 teaspoon salt
- 1 bay leaf
  Dash pepper
- ¼ cup dry white wine

In skillet combine onions, garlic, and water. Bring to boiling. Cover and simmer 10 minutes or till onion is tender. Drain. Add chicken to skillet. Combine tomatoes, tomato sauce, mushrooms, green pepper, basil, salt, bay leaf, and pepper. Pour over chicken. Cover and simmer for 30 minutes. Stir in wine. Cook, uncovered, 15 minutes more. Remove bay leaf. Skim excess fat from juices. Transfer chicken and sauce to serving platter. Makes 6 servings.

Creamy Chicken Salad
282/serving

- 1 teaspoon minced dried onion
- 2 tablespoons skim milk
- ½ cup plain yogurt
- 2 ounces Neufchâtel cheese, softened
- ¼ cup shredded Swiss cheese
- ½ teaspoon Worcestershire sauce
- ¾ cup chopped cooked chicken
- ¾ cup sliced celery
- ½ cup shredded carrot
  Lettuce
  Alfalfa sprouts

In large bowl soak dried onion in the milk for 5 minutes. Stir in yogurt, cheeses, Worcestershire sauce, and ¼ teaspoon *salt*. Stir in chicken, celery, and carrot. Chill. To serve, spoon chicken mixture onto lettuce-lined plates; top with alfalfa sprouts. Makes 2 servings.

Claypot Chicken
160/serving

- 1 tablespoon lemon juice
- 1 2½- to 3-pound broiler-fryer chicken, skinned
- 1 teaspoon dried marjoram, crushed
- ¼ teaspoon salt
  Paprika

Presoak a claypot lid and bottom in water for 10 minutes; drain. Sprinkle lemon juice over chicken. Combine marjoram, salt, and dash *pepper*; rub over outside of chicken. Tie chicken legs to tail; twist wing tips under back. Place chicken, breast side up, in pot. Sprinkle lightly with paprika. Cover tightly and place in unheated oven; set oven temperature at 400°. Bake for 1 hour or till chicken is tender. Season to taste. (*Or*, use a covered roaster instead of a claypot.) Makes 6 servings.

Vegetable-Stuffed Chicken Breasts—260/serving

2 whole medium chicken breasts, skinned, boned, and halved lengthwise
2½ c s sliced fresh mushrooms
2 tablespoons sliced green onion
2 tablespoons finely chopped celery
¼ teaspoon dried thyme, crushed
1 tablespoon butter or margarine
1½ teaspoons lemon juice
1 medium tomato, peeled, seeded, and chopped
2 tablespoons butter or margarine
¾ teaspoon instant chicken bouillon granules
  Skim milk
2 teaspoons cornstarch
  Dash dried thyme, crushed
1 tablespoon dry white wine

Place each chicken breast half between 2 pieces of clear plastic wrap; pound to ⅛-inch thickness. Remove wrap; season chicken with salt and pepper. Cook mushrooms, onion, celery, and ¼ teaspoon thyme in the 1 tablespoon butter or margarine till vegetables are tender and most of the liquid has evaporated. Remove from heat. Stir in lemon juice, ¼ teaspoon *salt*, and dash *pepper*. Gently stir in tomato. Spoon some of the mixture onto each chicken piece. Fold in sides; roll up jelly-roll style. Secure with wooden picks.

In skillet slowly brown chicken on all sides in 2 tablespoons butter. Add bouillon granules and ½ cup *water*. Cover; simmer for 20 minutes or till chicken is tender. Remove chicken; keep warm. Measure pan juices; add enough skim milk to measure ½ cup liquid. In screw-top jar combine milk mixture, cornstarch, dash thyme, and dash *salt*. Cover and shake till combined. Pour into skillet. Cook and stir till bubbly. Stir in wine. To serve, spoon sauce over chicken. Serves 4.

Chicken-Cauliflower Casseroles—249/serving

¼ cup chopped onion
1 cup skim milk
1 tablespoon cornstarch
1 teaspoon instant chicken bouillon granules
¼ cup shredded American cheese
½ of a 10-ounce package frozen cauliflower, cooked and drained
½ cup chopped cooked chicken
2 tablespoons chopped pimiento
¼ cup shredded American cheese

Combine onion and ¼ cup *water*. Bring to boiling. Cover and simmer for 5 minutes. Drain. Combine skim milk, cornstarch, bouillon granules, ¼ teaspoon *salt,* and dash *pepper*. Add to onion. Cook and stir till thickened and bubbly. Add ¼ cup cheese; stir to melt. Remove from heat. Halve any large pieces of cauliflower. Stir in cauliflower, chicken, and pimiento. Spoon mixture into 2 individual baking dishes. Bake in a 325° oven for 15 minutes. Sprinkle remaining cheese atop each. Bake 5 minutes more. Serve immediately. Serves 2.

Turkey-Fruit Salad 238/serving

8 cups torn spinach leaves
1 cup sliced celery
1 8-ounce can pineapple chunks (juice pack)
2 medium apples
1 orange, peeled and sectioned
½ pound cooked turkey, cut into strips
½ cup plain yogurt
2 tablespoons buttermilk
½ teaspoon celery seed
  Dash bottled hot pepper sauce

In salad bowl combine spinach and celery. Drain pineapple, reserving juice. Core apples; cut into wedges. Dip apple wedges in reserved pineapple juice. Arrange pineapple chunks, apple wedges, orange sections, and turkey atop spinach. For dressing combine yogurt, buttermilk, celery seed, and hot pepper sauce. Pass dressing. Makes 4 servings.

Garden Chicken Salad 183/serving

½ cup lemon yogurt
3 tablespoons skim milk
1 tablespoon snipped parsley
1 tablespoon tarragon vinegar
2 teaspoons Dijon-style mustard
½ teaspoon celery seed
¼ teaspoon salt
2 cups cubed cooked chicken or turkey
2 cups torn romaine
2 cups torn bibb lettuce
1 cup cauliflower flowerets
1 cup alfalfa sprouts
½ of a small red onion, sliced and separated into rings

For dressing, in small bowl combine yogurt, skim milk, parsley, vinegar, mustard, celery seed, and ¼ teaspoon salt. Chill.

Season chicken or turkey lightly with salt and pepper. On 4 individual salad plates, arrange chicken or turkey, romaine, bibb lettuce, cauliflower, alfalfa sprouts, and onion. Spoon dressing over each serving. Makes 4 servings.

Fresh fruits and vegetables enhance both the flavor and appearance of *Turkey-Fruit Salad* and *Garden Chicken Salad*.

Poultry

Chicken in Wine Sauce
267/serving

Chicken breasts simmer in a tomato-wine sauce—

- ½ cup chopped onion
- 2 tablespoons snipped parsley
- 1 clove garlic, minced
- ½ teaspoon dried marjoram, crushed
- 3 tablespoons butter *or* margarine
- 2 whole medium chicken breasts, skinned and halved lengthwise
- ⅔ cup tomato purée
- ⅓ cup dry red wine
- ⅓ cup water
- ½ teaspoon salt
- ⅛ teaspoon pepper
- 2 teaspoons cornstarch
- 1 tablespoon cold water
  Snipped parsley

In heavy skillet cook onion, the 2 tablespoons parsley, garlic, and marjoram in *1 tablespoon* butter or margarine till onion is tender but not brown. Remove from skillet and set aside. Add the remaining 2 tablespoons butter or margarine to skillet; brown chicken on all sides. Combine tomato purée, dry red wine, ⅓ cup water, salt, and pepper. Add to skillet along with the onion mixture. Cover and simmer for 45 minutes or till chicken is tender. Remove chicken to serving platter; keep warm. Spoon excess fat from sauce. Combine cornstarch and 1 tablespoon cold water; add to sauce in skillet. Cook and stir over medium heat till sauce is thickened and bubbly. Cook and stir 1 to 2 minutes more. To serve, pour sauce over chicken; sprinkle additional snipped parsley over all. Makes 4 servings.

Lemon Chicken Breasts
221/serving

- 3 whole medium chicken breasts, skinned, boned, and halved lengthwise
- 2 cups chopped fresh mushrooms
- ¼ cup sliced green onion
- 1 tablespoon butter *or* margarine
- ½ cup skim milk
- 2 teaspoons cornstarch
- ¼ teaspoon salt
- ¼ teaspoon dried thyme, crushed
  Dash pepper
- 1 tablespoon snipped parsley
- 2 teaspoons lemon juice
- 2 tablespoons butter *or* margarine
- ½ cup water
- 1½ teaspoons instant chicken bouillon granules
- 1 teaspoon lemon juice
- 1½ teaspoons cornstarch
- 2 tablespoons cold water

Place each chicken half between 2 pieces of plastic wrap and pound to ⅛-inch thickness. Remove wrap.

In saucepan cook mushrooms and onion in 1 tablespoon butter or margarine till onion is tender and most of the liquid is evaporated. Combine milk, 2 teaspoons cornstarch, salt, thyme, and pepper. Add to mushroom mixture. Cook and stir till thickened and bubbly. Cook and stir 2 minutes more. Remove from heat; stir in parsley and 2 teaspoons lemon juice. Cool without stirring. Spoon some of the mixture on each chicken piece. Fold in sides and roll up jelly-roll style. Secure with wooden picks.

In skillet brown chicken rolls in 2 tablespoons butter. Add ½ cup water, bouillon granules, and 1 teaspoon lemon juice. Cover and simmer for 20 minutes or till chicken is tender. Remove chicken to serving platter; remove wooden picks. Keep chicken warm while preparing sauce.

Skim fat from skillet juices. Measure pan juices; if necessary, add water to equal ¾ cup liquid. Return to skillet.

Combine cornstarch and 2 tablespoons cold water. Add to juices; cook and stir till thickened and bubbly. Cook 2 minutes more. Spoon sauce over chicken rolls. Serves 6.

Hawaiian Chicken
307/serving

- 1 8-ounce can pineapple chunks (juice pack)
- ¼ cup chopped onion
- 1 tablespoon brown sugar
- 1 tablespoon vinegar
- 1 tablespoon soy sauce
- 1 teaspoon instant chicken bouillon granules
- ¼ teaspoon salt
- 1 whole medium chicken breast, skinned and halved lengthwise
- 1½ teaspoons cornstarch
- 2 tablespoons cold water
- 1 11-ounce can mandarin orange sections, drained

Drain pineapple, reserving juice. Add enough water to juice to measure ½ cup liquid. Set pineapple aside. In skillet combine the pineapple liquid, onion, brown sugar, vinegar, soy sauce, bouillon granules, and salt. Bring to boiling. Add chicken; reduce heat. Tightly cover and simmer for 30 minutes or till chicken is tender. Remove chicken; set aside. Combine cornstarch and 2 tablespoons cold water; stir into skillet. Cook and stir till thickened and bubbly. Add pineapple, orange sections, and chicken; heat through. Spoon sauce over chicken. Makes 2 servings.

Chicken Livers Tarragon
248/serving

- 1 medium zucchini, thinly sliced
- ½ cup thinly sliced celery
- ½ cup chopped onion
- 1 tablespoon butter *or* margarine
- 1 pound chicken livers
- ¾ cup water
- ½ cup skim milk
- 1½ teaspoons instant beef bouillon granules
- ½ teaspoon dried tarragon, crushed
- ¼ teaspoon salt
  Dash pepper
- 1 tablespoon cornstarch
- 1 tablespoon cold water

In 10-inch skillet cook zucchini, celery, and onion in butter or margarine till tender. Add chicken livers; cook about 5 minutes or till just browned. Stir in ¾ cup water, the skim milk, bouillon granules, tarragon, salt, and pepper. Cover and simmer 5 minutes. Combine cornstarch and 1 tablespoon cold water; stir into liver mixture. Cook and stir till thickened and bubbly. Cook and stir 1 to 2 minutes more. Makes 4 servings.

Microwave directions: In a 2-quart nonmetal casserole, cook zucchini, celery, and onion in butter or margarine in countertop microwave oven on high power about 2 minutes or till vegetables are tender. Add livers to onion mixture. Stir in cornstarch; mix in ¾ cup water, the skim milk, bouillon granules, tarragon, salt, and pepper. Omit the 1 tablespoon cold water. Micro-cook, covered, for 6 minutes or till livers are barely pink, stirring after 3 minutes.

Turkey-Vegetable Bake
142/serving

- 1 cup chopped carrot
- 1 cup sliced celery
- ½ cup chopped onion
- ½ cup chopped green pepper
- 1½ cups chopped cooked turkey *or* chicken
- 1 4-ounce can sliced mushrooms, drained
- ½ teaspoon dried marjoram, crushed
- ¼ teaspoon ground sage
- ¼ teaspoon salt
  Dash pepper
- 2 beaten eggs
- ½ cup skim milk
- ¼ cup shredded cheddar cheese

In covered saucepan cook carrot, celery, onion, and green pepper in small amount boiling water for 10 minutes or till tender. Drain. In 8x8x2-inch baking pan combine vegetable mixture, turkey or chicken, mushrooms, marjoram, sage, salt, and pepper. In bowl combine eggs and milk; pour over turkey mixture. Sprinkle cheese atop. Bake in 325° oven 30 to 35 minutes or till set. Let stand 5 minutes. Cut into squares. Makes 6 servings.

Mandarin Chicken
282/serving

- 1 whole large chicken breast, skinned and boned (1 pound)
- 2 tablespoons soy sauce
- ½ teaspoon grated gingerroot
- 2 tablespoons cooking oil
- 1 8-ounce can water chestnuts, drained and thinly sliced
- ¾ cup bias-sliced celery
- ¼ cup water
- 1 tablespoon soy sauce
- 2 teaspoons cornstarch
- ¼ teaspoon instant chicken bouillon granules
- 1 orange, peeled and sectioned

Cut chicken into 1-inch pieces. Combine 2 tablespoons soy sauce and the gingerroot; add chicken. Let stand for 20 minutes. Heat *1 tablespoon* of the oil in wok or large skillet; add water chestnuts and celery. Stir-fry for 1 to 2 minutes or till celery is crisp-tender. Remove from wok or skillet. Heat remaining oil in wok; add chicken mixture and stir-fry for 2 to 3 minutes or till done. Return vegetables to wok. Combine water, 1 tablespoon soy sauce, cornstarch, and bouillon granules. Stir into wok. Cook and stir till bubbly. Add orange sections. Cover; cook for 1 minute more. Makes 3 servings.

Stir-Fried Chicken with Almonds—357/serving

- 1½ pounds chicken breasts, skinned and boned
- ⅓ cup chicken broth
- 2 tablespoons soy sauce
- 4 teaspoons cornstarch
- 2 tablespoons cooking oil
- ¼ cup sliced almonds
- 6 green onions, bias sliced into 1-inch pieces
- 1 6-ounce package frozen pea pods, thawed
- 2 cups sliced fresh mushrooms

Cut chicken into 1-inch pieces. Stir chicken broth and soy sauce into cornstarch; set aside.

In wok or skillet heat oil over high heat. Add almonds and stir-fry 1 minute or till just brown. Remove almonds. Add chicken and stir-fry 2 to 3 minutes or till done; remove chicken. Add green onion and pea pods and stir-fry 1 minute; remove vegetables. Add mushrooms and stir-fry 1 minute. Stir broth mixture; add to mushrooms. Cook and stir till bubbly. Stir in chicken and pea pod mixture. Cover; cook 1 minute. Stir in almonds. Makes 6 servings.

Main Dishes
Fish & Seafood

Main Dish Tuna Toss
167/serving

- ½ cup plain yogurt
- 3 tablespoons chili sauce
  Skim milk
- 8 cups torn salad greens
- 1 6½-ounce can tuna (water pack), drained
- 2 hard-cooked eggs, sliced
- 1 small red onion, sliced and separated into rings
- ½ cup sliced pimiento-stuffed olives
- 3 tablespoons chopped canned green chili peppers

For dressing, combine yogurt and chili sauce. Add a little skim milk if necessary to make desired consistency. Chill. In salad bowl combine torn salad greens, tuna, hard-cooked egg slices, onion, olives, and chili peppers. Pour dressing over all; toss to coat. Makes 4 servings.

Marinated Tuna and Vegetables—245/serving

- 2 large carrots, cut into 2-inch-long julienne strips
- ½ small head cauliflower, broken into flowerets (1½ cups)
- 1 10-ounce package frozen peas
- ½ cup thinly sliced celery
- ¼ cup sliced green onion
- 1 6½-ounce can tuna (water pack), well drained
- ¾ cup Tomato Salad Dressing (see recipe, page 75)

Cook carrots and cauliflower together in small amount of boiling salted water for 10 minutes. Add peas. Cook 5 minutes more or till all vegetables are crisp-tender. Drain. In bowl combine cooked vegetables, celery, and green onion. Add tuna and Tomato Salad Dressing; toss. Cover and chill before serving. Makes 3 servings.

Salmon-Stuffed Tomatoes
273/serving

- 1 cup dairy sour cream
- ¼ cup chopped cucumber
- ¼ cup skim milk
- 1 tablespoon lemon juice
- 2 teaspoons snipped fresh dillweed or ½ teaspoon dried dillweed
- ¼ teaspoon salt
- 3 fresh artichokes or one 9-ounce package frozen artichoke hearts
- 1 tablespoon lemon juice
- 1 15½-ounce can salmon, drained and broken into chunks
- 1 cup sliced fresh mushrooms
- 3 hard-cooked eggs, chopped
- ¼ teaspoon salt
  Dash pepper
- 6 large tomatoes, chilled

For dressing, combine sour cream, cucumber, milk, 1 tablespoon lemon juice, dillweed, and ¼ teaspoon salt. Chill.

Add fresh whole artichokes to large amount of boiling salted water; add 1 tablespoon lemon juice. Cover; reduce heat and simmer about 20 to 30 minutes or till stem is tender and leaf pulls easily from the base. Drain and cool. Pull off outer leaves; scoop out choke. Chop remaining heart into pieces. (Or, cook frozen artichoke hearts according to package directions; drain and chop. Omit the 1 tablespoon lemon juice.) In mixing bowl combine chopped artichoke hearts, salmon, mushrooms, egg, ¼ teaspoon salt, and pepper; chill.

Starting at top, and cutting to, but not through base of tomato, cut each tomato into quarters. Place on serving plate and spread wedges open; fill with salmon mixture. Spoon dressing over. Garnish with fresh dill, if desired. Makes 6 servings.

Salmon-Cauliflower Casserole—222/serving

- 1 10-ounce package frozen cauliflower
- ¼ cup chopped onion
- 1 tablespoon butter or margarine
- 1 10¾-ounce can condensed cream of celery soup
- 1 4-ounce can chopped mushrooms, drained
- ½ cup grated Parmesan cheese
- 1 tablespoon lemon juice
- ½ teaspoon dried dillweed
- 1 7¾-ounce can pink salmon, drained and broken into chunks
  Lemon twist

In covered saucepan cook cauliflower in a small amount of boiling salted water for 3 minutes. Drain; cut cauliflower into small pieces. Set aside. In saucepan cook onion in butter till tender. Remove from heat. Stir in condensed soup, mushrooms, *half* of the Parmesan cheese, lemon juice, dillweed, and dash *pepper*. Fold in salmon and cauliflower. Turn mixture into a 1-quart casserole. Sprinkle remaining cheese atop. Bake, uncovered, in a 350° oven for 25 to 30 minutes or till heated through. Garnish with lemon twist. Serves 4.

Microwave directions: Place unwrapped package of cauliflower atop paper toweling in countertop microwave oven. Micro-cook on high power for 3 to 4 minutes. Cut cauliflower into small pieces. In a 1-quart nonmetal casserole micro-cook onion in butter, uncovered, 2 minutes or till onion is tender. Stir in condensed soup, mushrooms, *half* of the cheese, lemon juice, dillweed, and dash *pepper*. Stir in salmon and cauliflower. Micro-cook, uncovered, for 3 minutes; stir mixture. Micro-cook 2 to 3 minutes more or till heated through. Stir; sprinkle with remaining cheese and with *paprika*.

Vegetable-Sauced Fish Fillets—193/serving

4 fresh *or* frozen fish fillets (1 pound)
1 medium tomato, peeled, seeded, and chopped
3 tablespoons finely chopped celery
2 tablespoons snipped parsley
2 tablespoons thinly sliced green onion
½ teaspoon salt
¼ teaspoon dried rosemary, crushed
2 teaspoons butter *or* margarine
¼ cup water
¼ cup dry white wine
¼ teaspoon Worcestershire sauce
1 tablespoon cold water
2 teaspoons cornstarch

Thaw fish, if frozen. Arrange fish fillets in a single layer in a 10-inch skillet. Combine chopped tomato, celery, parsley, green onion, salt, and rosemary. Top fillets with the tomato mixture. Dot each fillet with *½ teaspoon* of the butter or margarine. Combine ¼ cup water, wine, and Worcestershire sauce; pour into skillet. Cover and simmer for 10 to 12 minutes or till fish flakes easily when tested with a fork. Remove fish to serving platter; keep warm. Strain pan juices; measure ¾ cup juices. Combine 1 tablespoon cold water and the cornstarch; stir into skillet with the reserved ¾ cup pan juices. Cook and stir over medium heat till thickened and bubbly. Cook 1 minute more. Spoon sauce over fish. Serve immediately. Makes 4 servings.

Cooking Fish

Whether broiled, baked, steamed, or poached, fish is an excellent quick-cooking, low-caloried main dish. To determine which cooking method to use, check the fat content of the fish.

"Fat" fish have oil throughout the flesh; "lean" fish have a drier flesh. Fat fish can be broiled or baked because their fat helps keep them from drying out during cooking. Lean fish generally are steamed or poached to keep the flesh moist. However, lean fish can be baked or broiled if basted with a little melted butter or margarine.

Fat fish include lake trout, whitefish, eel, mackerel, salmon, and tuna. Lean fish include catfish, perch, cod, flounder, sole, and red snapper.

The size of the fish pieces also help determine the cooking method. Thin fillets are best broiled, whereas thicker steaks and pan-dressed fish are better poached or baked.

During cooking, doneness is indicated by a change in flesh color from a translucent pinkish white to an opaque white. To check for doneness, place fork tines into the fish at a 45-degree angle and twist the fork. If the fish resists flaking and still looks translucent, it is not done. At the just-right stage, the fish will flake apart easily when the fork is twisted. It also will have a milky white color. If cooked too long, fish becomes mealy, tough, and dry.

Grapefruit-Sole Salad 178/serving

3 cups shredded lettuce
½ pound sole fillets, cooked, flaked, and chilled
2 grapefruits, peeled and sectioned
½ cup chopped celery
½ cup Tomato Salad Dressing (see recipe, page 75)

Arrange lettuce on bottom of a salad bowl. Place fish, grapefruit sections, and celery atop. Drizzle Tomato Salad Dressing over all. Serve immediately. Makes 3 servings.

Baked Red Snapper 162/serving

2 pounds fresh *or* frozen red snapper fillets *or* other fish fillets
2 tablespoons lemon juice
½ cup chopped celery
½ cup chopped onion
¼ cup chopped green pepper
¾ cup vegetable juice cocktail

Thaw fish, if frozen. Place fish in greased baking pan. Season with salt and pepper. Drizzle lemon juice over fish. Bake fish in a 350° oven for 10 minutes. Meanwhile, prepare sauce. In saucepan combine celery, onion, green pepper, and vegetable juice cocktail. Simmer, uncovered, for 10 minutes. Remove fish from oven. Drain off all excess liquid. Pour the simmered vegetable sauce over fish. Return fish to oven and bake 15 minutes more or till fish flakes easily when tested with a fork, basting with the vegetable sauce occasionally. Makes 6 servings.

Rice-Vegetable Stuffed Fish—305/serving

Use *quick-cooking* rice because it is low in calories—

- 1   1½-pound fresh *or* frozen pan-dressed white-fleshed fish (with head and tail)
- ½   cup quick-cooking rice
- 1   4-ounce can sliced mushrooms, drained
- ½   cup sliced celery
- ½   cup thinly sliced carrot
- ¼   cup sliced green onion
- 2   tablespoons butter *or* margarine
- 1   tablespoon snipped parsley
- 1   tablespoon lemon juice
- ¾   teaspoon salt
- ½   teaspoon dried marjoram, crushed
- ¼   teaspoon pepper
- 2   teaspoons butter *or* margarine, melted
- 1   teaspoon lemon juice

Thaw fish, if frozen. Prepare rice according to package directions, *except* omit the butter or margarine. In saucepan cook mushrooms, celery, carrot, and onion in the 2 tablespoons butter or margarine till vegetables are tender. Stir in parsley, 1 tablespoon lemon juice, ¾ teaspoon salt, marjoram, and pepper. Stir in the cooked rice.

Sprinkle fish cavity with salt. Spoon rice-vegetable mixture into fish. Skewer fish closed; place in a greased shallow baking pan. Combine the 2 teaspoons melted butter or margarine and 1 teaspoon lemon juice; brush over fish. Bake, uncovered, in a 350° oven about 25 minutes or till fish flakes easily when tested with a fork. Transfer fish and stuffing to serving platter. Makes 4 servings.

Poached Halibut with Spinach—268/serving

pictured on pages 24 and 25

- 1   10-ounce package frozen chopped spinach
- ¼   teaspoon ground nutmeg
- 4   cups water
- ⅓   cup lemon juice
- 1   small onion, sliced
- ¼   cup chopped celery
- ¼   teaspoon salt
- ⅛   teaspoon pepper
- 4   halibut steaks (about 1⅓ pounds total)
- ¼   cup grated Parmesan cheese
     Lemon wedges

Cook spinach according to package directions. Drain well; stir in nutmeg. In a 10-inch skillet combine water, lemon juice, onion, celery, salt, and pepper. Simmer 5 minutes. Add fish; simmer, covered, 5 to 10 minutes or till fish flakes easily when tested with a fork. Carefully remove fish to a 12x7½x2-inch baking dish or a broiler-proof platter. Spread spinach over each halibut steak. Sprinkle cheese atop each. Broil fish portions 4 to 5 inches from heat for 1 to 2 minutes. Garnish with lemon wedges. Makes 4 servings.

Marinated Sole—173/serving

- 1   pound fresh *or* frozen sole fillets
- ½   cup unsweetened pineapple juice
- 2   tablespoons snipped parsley
- 1   tablespoon lemon juice
- 2   teaspoons Worcestershire sauce
- 1   teaspoon minced dried onion
- ½   teaspoon dry mustard
- ¼   teaspoon salt

Thaw fish, if frozen. Separate into fillets; place in plastic bag in bowl. Combine pineapple juice, parsley, lemon juice, Worcestershire sauce, minced dried onion, dry mustard, and salt. Pour over fish in bag. Marinate in refrigerator for 6 hours. Drain fish, reserving marinade. Place fillets on unheated rack of broiler pan. Turn under any thin edges. Broil 4 inches from heat for 4 to 5 minutes or till fish flakes easily when tested with a fork, brushing occasionally with marinade. Makes 4 servings.

Baked Curried Fish 184/serving

See tip, page 53 for types of fish to use—

- 1½   pounds fresh *or* frozen fish fillets
- 2   medium onions, thinly sliced
- 1   cup sliced celery
- 1   teaspoon curry powder
- 1   tablespoon butter *or* margarine
- ¼   cup skim milk
- ¾   teaspoon salt

Thaw fish, if frozen. In small covered saucepan cook onion, celery, and curry powder in butter or margarine over medium heat 8 to 10 minutes or till onion is tender. Remove from heat. Stir in milk. Place fish in a lightly greased 12x7½x2-inch baking dish. Sprinkle with the salt. Spoon vegetables over fish. Bake, uncovered, in 350° oven for 25 minutes or till fish flakes easily when tested with a fork. Makes 6 servings.

Mushrooms, celery, carrot, onion, and rice flavor and color *Rice-Vegetable Stuffed Fish.* ▷

Main Dishes
Fish & Seafood

Cleaning Shrimp

Before cooking fresh or frozen shrimp, remove the sandy black vein that runs along the back of the shrimp. To do so, use a sharp knife to make a shallow slit along the back of the shrimp, then use the knife's tip to scrape out the vein. Some shrimp may be already deveined when purchased.

Spicy Shrimp Skillet
209/serving

- 1 pound fresh *or* frozen shrimp in shells
- 2 tablespoons cooking oil
- 2 cups chopped onion
- 2 cloves garlic, minced
- 1 teaspoon grated gingerroot
- ⅛ teaspoon cayenne
- 1 bay leaf
- 1 tablespoon water
- ½ teaspoon ground coriander
- ½ of a 9-ounce package frozen cut green beans, cooked and drained
- 2 tablespoons vinegar
- ½ teaspoon salt

Thaw shrimp, if frozen. Shell and devein shrimp. Heat oil in a 10-inch skillet. Add onion, garlic, gingerroot, cayenne, and bay leaf; cook and stir 3 to 5 minutes. Add water and coriander. Cook and stir 3 to 5 minutes more. (Add more water by teaspoons, if needed, to keep spice mixture moist.) Add shrimp, green beans, vinegar, and salt. Cook and stir for 5 minutes or till shrimp is just tender. Remove bay leaf before serving shrimp. Makes 4 servings.

Vegetable-Topped Halibut Steaks—272/serving

- 1 12-ounce package frozen halibut steaks
  Lemon juice
- ½ teaspoon salt
- 2 medium carrots, shredded (1 cup)
- 2 tablespoons sliced green onion
- 2 tablespoons snipped parsley
- ½ teaspoon dried marjoram, crushed
- 1 small tomato, cut into wedges and seeded

Thaw fish. Place in a 10x6x2-inch baking dish; brush with a little lemon juice and sprinkle with the salt. Toss together carrot, onion, parsley, and marjoram; spoon atop fish. Top with tomato wedges. Bake, covered, in 350° oven for 25 to 30 minutes or till fish flakes easily when tested with a fork. With a slotted spatula, carefully lift fish and vegetables to platter. Makes 2 servings.

Microwave directions: Arrange fish and vegetables as above in a nonmetal casserole. Cover with clear plastic wrap. Cook in a countertop microwave oven on high power about 5 minutes or till fish flakes easily, turning dish after 2½ minutes. Serve as above.

Shrimp Kebabs
169/serving

- 1 pound fresh *or* frozen large shrimp in shells
- 1 8-ounce can pineapple slices (juice pack)
- 3 tablespoons lemon juice
- 2 teaspoons cooking oil
- ½ teaspoon dry mustard
- ¼ teaspoon pepper
  Few dashes bottled hot pepper sauce
- 8 cherry tomatoes

Thaw shrimp, if frozen. Shell and devein shrimp. Drain pineapple, reserving juice. Halve pineapple slices. Combine reserved pineapple juice, lemon juice, cooking oil, dry mustard, pepper, hot pepper sauce, and ½ teaspoon *salt*; pour over shrimp. Cover; refrigerate 2 hours, spooning marinade over shrimp occasionally. Drain shrimp, reserving marinade. On 4 skewers alternate shrimp and pineapple slices. Broil 4 inches from heat for 4 minutes, brushing occasionally with marinade. Turn kebabs; put two cherry tomatoes on the end of each skewer. Broil about 4 minutes more, brushing with marinade. Serves 4.

Shrimp Stack-Ups
176/serving

pictured on pages 24 and 25

- 2 4½-ounce cans shrimp, drained and chopped
- 2 hard-cooked eggs
- 2 tablespoons chopped celery
- 2 tablespoons chopped sweet pickle
- 2 tablespoons thinly sliced green onion
- ½ cup plain yogurt
- ¼ cup cream-style cottage cheese
- 1 tablespoon lemon juice
  Lettuce leaves
- 12 tomato slices
- 6 slices bread, toasted and quartered

Rinse shrimp. Chop eggs, reserving one yolk. Cover and chill reserved yolk. In a small bowl combine shrimp, chopped eggs, celery, sweet pickle, and onion. Stir together yogurt, cottage cheese, lemon juice, and dash *pepper*; add to shrimp mixture. Mix lightly and chill. To serve, on 6 individual lettuce-lined plates place two tomato slices. Spoon about ½ cup shrimp mixture atop tomato slices on each plate. Sieve the reserved yolk; sprinkle some atop each mound of shrimp. Accompany with toast quarters. Serves 6.

Wild Rice Shrimp Creole
229/serving

- 1 pound fresh *or* frozen shrimp in shells
- ½ cup chopped onion
- ⅓ cup chopped green pepper
- 2 tablespoons butter *or* margarine
- 1 28-ounce can tomatoes, cut up
- 1¾ cups water
- ½ teaspoon salt
- ¼ teaspoon garlic salt
- ¼ teaspoon dried rosemary, crushed
- ¼ teaspoon paprika
- ¼ teaspoon pepper
- 1 6-ounce package regular long grain and wild rice mix
-    Bottled hot pepper sauce

Thaw shrimp, if frozen. Shell and devein shrimp. In 3-quart saucepan cook onion and green pepper in butter or margarine about 5 minutes or till tender. Add *undrained* tomatoes, water, and seasonings. Stir in *both* packets from rice mix. Cover; simmer 20 minutes. Add shrimp. Cover; simmer 10 minutes more. Pass hot pepper sauce. Makes 6 servings.

Shrimp and Pepper Stir-Fry
226/serving

- ¾ pound fresh *or* frozen shelled shrimp
- ½ teaspoon instant chicken bouillon granules
- ⅓ cup hot water
- 1 teaspoon cornstarch
- ⅛ teaspoon pepper
- 1 tablespoon lemon juice
- 2 teaspoons soy sauce
- 2 tablespoons cooking oil
- ½ cup bias-sliced green onions
- 1 large green pepper, cut into 1-inch pieces
- 1⅓ cups hot cooked rice

Thaw shrimp, if frozen. (Halve large shrimp lengthwise.) Dissolve bouillon granules in the hot water. Combine cornstarch and pepper; stir in lemon juice and soy sauce. Stir in bouillon. Set aside.

Heat wok or large skillet over high heat; add oil. Add onion and green pepper; stir-fry 2 to 3 minutes. Remove from wok. Add shrimp; stir-fry 2 to 4 minutes or till done. Stir in lemon juice mixture; cook till thickened and bubbly. Add vegetables. Cover and cook 1 minute. Serve with rice. Makes 4 servings.

Creamed Crab with Tomato
280/serving

- 1 cup sliced fresh mushrooms
- ½ cup sliced green onion
- ¼ cup finely chopped celery
- 1 tablespoon butter *or* margarine
- 1¾ cups skim milk
- 2 tablespoons cornstarch
- ½ teaspoon salt
- ½ teaspoon dried thyme, crushed
- ¼ teaspoon pepper
- 1 cup shredded process Swiss cheese
- 1 7-ounce can crab meat, drained, flaked, and cartilage removed
- 1 medium tomato, peeled, seeded, and chopped
- 2 slices bread, toasted and quartered

In saucepan cook mushrooms, onion, and celery in butter or margarine till onion is tender. Stir together milk, cornstarch, salt, thyme, and pepper. Add to onion mixture all at once. Cook and stir till thickened and bubbly. Stir in Swiss cheese till melted. Carefully stir in crab and chopped tomato. Heat through. Serve over toast quarters. Makes 4 servings.

Newburg-Style Crab
278/serving

- 1 tablespoon butter *or* margarine
- 1 tablespoon cornstarch
- 1¼ cups skim milk
- 2 beaten egg yolks
- 1 6-ounce package frozen crab meat, thawed
- ½ of a 10-ounce package frozen peas, cooked and drained
- 3 tablespoons dry white wine
- 2 teaspoons lemon juice
- 6 Whole Wheat Biscuit Crackers (see recipe, page 92)

Melt butter; stir in cornstarch and ¼ teaspoon *salt*. Add milk all at once. Cook and stir till bubbly. Cook and stir 2 minutes more. Stir *half* of the hot mixture into yolks. Return to hot mixture in saucepan. Cook and stir till bubbly. Add crab and peas; heat through. Stir in wine and lemon juice. Serve over Whole Wheat Biscuit Crackers. Serves 3.

Oriental Scallops
120/serving

- ¾ pound fresh *or* frozen scallops
- 2 tablespoons soy sauce
- 1 tablespoon lemon juice
- ½ teaspoon ground ginger
- ¼ teaspoon dry mustard
- 8 cherry tomatoes
- 1 medium green pepper, cut into 1-inch squares

Thaw scallops, if frozen. Place in a shallow glass dish. Combine soy sauce, lemon juice, ginger, and dry mustard; pour over scallops. Cover; let stand at room temperature 1 hour. Drain, reserving marinade. On 4 skewers, alternate scallops, tomatoes, and green pepper. Place on unheated rack of broiler pan. Broil 5 inches from heat for 7 to 8 minutes per side, basting occasionally with marinade. Serves 4.

Main Dishes
Eggs & Cheese

Spicy Poached Egg Stacks
271/serving

- 1 teaspoon minced dried onion
- 1 6-ounce can vegetable juice cocktail (⅔ cup)
- 2 teaspoons cornstarch
- ¼ teaspoon dried marjoram, crushed
  Dash salt
  Dash bottled hot pepper sauce
- 4 slices Canadian-style bacon, cut ¼ inch thick
- 4 eggs
- 2 English muffins, split and toasted

In saucepan soften onion in the vegetable juice cocktail for 5 minutes. Stir in cornstarch. Add marjoram, salt, and hot pepper sauce. Cook and stir till mixture is thickened and bubbly. Keep sauce warm.

In skillet heat Canadian-style bacon over medium heat about 5 minutes. Keep warm.

Lightly grease a 10-inch skillet. Break one egg into sauce dish. Heat about 1½ inches of water in skillet; bring to boiling. Reduce heat to simmer. Carefully slide egg into water. Repeat with remaining eggs. Simmer, uncovered, over low heat for 3 to 5 minutes. Do not let water boil. Smooth edges of eggs during cooking by using a spoon to gently pull away any trailing strings of egg white. When eggs are cooked to desired doneness, remove with slotted spoon.

Place a slice of Canadian-style bacon atop each English muffin half. Top each with a poached egg. Spoon on vegetable sauce. Serve immediately. Makes 4 servings.

Vegetable-Filled Omelet
246/serving

pictured on pages 24 and 25

- 1 medium zucchini, thinly sliced
- ½ cup sliced fresh mushrooms
- ¼ cup sliced green onion
- ¼ cup chopped green pepper
- 1 7½-ounce can tomatoes, cut up
- ½ teaspoon dried basil, crushed
- ¼ teaspoon sugar
- 2 teaspoons cornstarch
- 8 eggs
- ¼ cup water
- 2 tablespoons butter or margarine

For filling, in saucepan cook zucchini, mushrooms, green onion, and green pepper in a small amount of boiling salted water about 5 minutes or till vegetables are crisp-tender. Drain well. Add undrained tomatoes, basil, sugar, and ½ teaspoon salt. Bring to boiling; reduce heat. Combine cornstarch and 1 tablespoon cold water; add to tomato mixture. Cook and stir till thickened and bubbly. Keep filling warm while preparing omelets.

To make omelets, beat together eggs, water, ½ teaspoon salt, and ⅛ teaspoon pepper till blended but not frothy. In a 6- or 8-inch skillet with flared sides heat ¼ of the butter or margarine till it sizzles and browns slightly. (Use less butter for pan with non-stick surface.) Lift and tilt the pan to coat the sides. Add ¼ of the egg mixture (about ½ cup); cook over medium heat. As eggs set, run spatula around edge, lifting eggs to allow uncooked portion to flow underneath. When eggs are set but still shiny, remove from heat. Spoon ¼ of the filling mixture (about ⅓ cup) across center. Fold ⅓ of omelet over center. Overlap remaining third atop filling; slide omelet out onto serving plate. Keep warm. Repeat to make 3 more omelets. Makes 4 servings.

Taco Scrambled Eggs
287/serving

- 6 beaten eggs
- ½ cup reconstituted nonfat dry milk
- ½ cup shredded cheddar cheese
- ½ teaspoon salt
  Few dashes bottled hot pepper sauce
- ½ cup chopped onion
- ¼ cup chopped canned green chili peppers
- 2 tablespoons butter or margarine
- 2 medium tomatoes, peeled, seeded, and chopped
  Shredded lettuce (optional)
- ⅔ cup plain yogurt
- 2 teaspoons chili powder

In bowl combine eggs, milk, cheese, salt, and hot pepper sauce. In skillet cook onion and green chili peppers in butter or margarine till onion is tender but not brown. Add the egg mixture. Cook without stirring till egg mixture begins to set on bottom and around edges. Lift and fold the partially cooked eggs with a spatula so uncooked portion flows underneath. Continue cooking 5 to 8 minutes or till eggs are cooked throughout but still glossy and moist. Add the chopped tomato. Cover and cook 1 minute. Serve eggs on shredded lettuce, if desired. Combine yogurt and chili powder; pass to dollop atop eggs and lettuce. Serve eggs immediately. Makes 4 servings.

Try both of these egg dishes with a south-of-the-border savor: *Spicy Poached Egg Stacks* and *Taco Scrambled Eggs*. ▷

Main Dishes
Eggs & Cheese

Cheese Soufflé—282/serving

4 eggs
¼ cup sliced green onion
1 clove garlic, minced
1 tablespoon butter *or* margarine
2 tablespoons cornstarch
½ teaspoon dried basil, crushed
¼ teaspoon salt
Dash cayenne
¾ cup skim milk
1¼ cups shredded sharp cheddar cheese (5 ounces)

Place a buttered foil collar on an ungreased 1½-quart soufflé dish, extending 2 inches above dish. Secure the foil strip using tape or a piece of string.

Separate the eggs; set aside. In a heavy saucepan cook onion and garlic in butter or margarine till onion is tender. Stir in cornstarch, basil, salt, and cayenne. Add the milk all at once; cook and stir over medium heat till thickened and bubbly. Add cheese; stir till melted. Remove from heat; set aside. In small mixer bowl beat the egg yolks till thick and lemon-colored (about 4 minutes). Slowly add the cheese mixture to egg yolks, stirring constantly. Wash beaters thoroughly.

Using clean beaters and large mixer bowl, beat egg whites till stiff peaks form. Gradually pour the egg yolk mixture over beaten whites; fold to blend. Pour into prepared soufflé dish.

For a top hat that puffs in the oven, use a knife to trace a 1-inch-deep circle through the mixture about 1 inch from edge. Bake in 300° oven about 1 hour or till knife inserted near center comes out clean. Serve immediately by breaking apart with two forks. Makes 4 servings.

Cheesy Strata—208/serving

3 cups dry bread cubes (about 4 slices bread)
1½ cups shredded process cheese spread *or* American cheese (6 ounces)
4 beaten eggs
1¾ cups skim milk
1 tablespoon finely chopped onion
½ teaspoon salt
¼ teaspoon dry mustard

Place *2 cups* of the bread cubes in an 8x8x2-inch baking pan. Top with shredded cheese, then with remaining bread cubes. Thoroughly stir together eggs, milk, onion, salt, and dry mustard. Pour evenly over mixture in pan. Cover; chill several hours or overnight. Bake, uncovered, in 325° oven about 40 minutes or till knife inserted near center comes out clean. Let stand 5 minutes before serving. Makes 6 servings.

Crab and Egg Casserole 233/serving

4 ounces Neufchâtel cheese
5 beaten eggs
1 cup skim milk
½ teaspoon salt
Dash pepper
1 6-ounce can crab meat, drained, flaked, and cartilage removed
½ cup finely chopped celery

In small mixer bowl beat cheese till softened and fluffy. Combine eggs, milk, salt, and pepper. Gradually add to cheese; beat till blended. Stir in crab and celery. Turn into a buttered 9-inch pie plate or quiche dish. Bake in 325° oven for 15 minutes; stir. Continue baking for 10 to 15 minutes or till knife inserted near center comes out clean. Makes 4 servings.

Broccoli-Yogurt Omelet 237/serving

½ of a 10-ounce package frozen chopped broccoli *or* 1 cup chopped fresh broccoli
¼ cup sliced green onion
⅓ cup plain yogurt
1 teaspoon cornstarch
¼ teaspoon dried basil, crushed
Dash pepper
5 eggs
2 tablespoons water
½ teaspoon salt
⅛ teaspoon pepper
2 tablespoons butter *or* margarine

In saucepan combine broccoli and onion. Cook according to broccoli package directions. (*Or*, cook fresh broccoli and onion in small amount boiling salted water about 10 minutes or till tender.) Drain broccoli and onion thoroughly. In saucepan combine yogurt, cornstarch, basil, and dash pepper. Stir in cooked broccoli. Heat through stirring constantly just till bubbly; keep warm.

For omelets beat together eggs, 2 tablespoons water, salt, and ⅛ teaspoon pepper. In 6-inch skillet with flared sides, heat ⅓ of the butter till it sizzles and browns slightly. Lift and tilt the pan to coat the sides. Add ⅓ of the egg mixture; cook over medium heat. As eggs set, run a spatula around edge of skillet lifting eggs to allow uncooked portion to flow underneath. When eggs are set but still shiny, remove from heat. Spoon ⅓ of the broccoli mixture across center. Fold ⅓ of omelet over center. Overlap remaining third atop filling. Slide omelet out onto hot plate. Keep omelet warm. Repeat to make 2 more omelets. Makes 3 servings.

Cheese-Cauliflower Chowder
266/serving

- ½ cup chopped onion
- 1¼ cups water
- 1 10-ounce package frozen cauliflower
- 1 4-ounce can sliced mushrooms
- 2 teaspoons instant chicken bouillon granules
- ½ teaspoon dry mustard
- ¾ cup skim milk
- 4 teaspoons cornstarch
- 2 cups shredded American cheese (8 ounces)
- 2 tablespoons chopped pimiento

In saucepan cook onion in water till tender. Add cauliflower, *undrained* mushrooms, bouillon granules, and dry mustard. Bring to boiling. Reduce heat; cover and simmer about 8 minutes or till cauliflower is just tender.

In screw-top jar combine milk and cornstarch; shake well. Stir into hot vegetable mixture. Cook and stir over medium heat till thickened and bubbly. Stir in shredded cheese and pimiento. Heat through, stirring to melt cheese. Makes 4 servings.

Individual Crustless Quiches
225/serving

- 1 4-ounce package sliced dried beef
- ½ of a medium onion, thinly sliced
- 3 beaten eggs
- 1½ cups skim milk
- 2 teaspoons all-purpose flour
- ¼ teaspoon salt
  Dash ground nutmeg
- ¾ cup shredded Swiss cheese (3 ounces)

Finely chop the sliced dried beef; set aside. In skillet cook sliced onion in a small amount of boiling water till tender; drain. In bowl thoroughly stir together the eggs, milk, flour, salt, and nutmeg. Stir in the chopped dried beef, onion, and cheese; mix well. Place four 10-ounce custard cups in a 13x9x2-inch baking pan; pour egg mixture into the custard cups. Place pan on oven rack; pour hot water into pan around custard cups to depth of 1 inch. Bake in 325° oven about 30 minutes or till knife inserted near center comes out clean. Let stand about 5 minutes before serving. Makes 4 servings.

Egg Salad Stuffed Tomatoes
184/serving

- 3 hard-cooked eggs, chopped
- ¼ cup plain yogurt
- ¼ cup dry cottage cheese
- 2 tablespoons finely chopped celery
- 2 tablespoons thinly sliced green onion
- ½ teaspoon dry mustard
- ¼ teaspoon salt
  Dash cayenne
- 2 medium tomatoes
- 1 tablespoon snipped parsley
  Lettuce

In bowl combine eggs, yogurt, cottage cheese, celery, green onion, dry mustard, salt, and cayenne. Cover and chill. For tomato shells, cut a slice off the top of each tomato. Scoop out seeds and flesh. Invert tomatoes on paper toweling to drain. Chill. To serve, sprinkle inside of tomatoes with salt and pepper. Spoon *half* of the egg mixture into each tomato shell. Sprinkle with snipped parsley. Arrange tomatoes on lettuce-lined plates. Makes 2 servings.

Poached Eggs with Cheese Sauce—197/serving

- ½ cup skim milk
- ½ teaspoon cornstarch
- ¼ teaspoon salt
- ¼ teaspoon dry mustard
- 1 beaten egg yolk
- ½ cup shredded American cheese
- 1 2-ounce can mushroom stems and pieces, drained and chopped
- 4 eggs
- 2 slices whole wheat bread, toasted and quartered

In saucepan combine milk, cornstarch, salt, and dry mustard. Cook and stir over medium heat till thickened and bubbly. Cook and stir 2 minutes more. Stir *half* of the hot mixture into the beaten yolk; return all to saucepan. Add cheese and mushrooms. Stir over low heat 2 to 3 minutes or till thickened and cheese is melted. Keep sauce warm.

To poach eggs, lightly grease a 10-inch skillet. Heat about 1½-inches of water in skillet to boiling. Reduce heat to simmer. Break one egg into a sauce dish. Carefully slide egg into water, holding lip of dish as close to water as possible. Repeat with remaining eggs so each has about ¼ of the space. Simmer, uncovered, over low heat for 3 to 5 minutes or till eggs are cooked to desired doneness. During cooking, smooth the edges of eggs by using a spoon to gently pull away any strings of trailing cooked egg white. Lift eggs out of water using a slotted spoon. Place 1 egg atop 2 toast quarters. Spoon some cheese sauce over each. Makes 4 servings.

Calorie-Trimmed
Side Dishes

Vegetables, salads, and salad dressings
receive special treatment in this chapter.
Pictured (from left): *Pineapple Carrots,
Marinated Tomato-Vegetable Salad*, steamed
cauliflower and broccoli, *Tomato Salad
Dressing*, and *Stuffed Potatoes*. (See index
for recipe pages.)

Calorie-Trimmed Side Dishes

Instead of thinking of vegetable and salad side dishes simply as plate fillers, think of them as nutritional and flavorful complements to protein main dishes.

A generous amount of vegetables in your diet contributes to sound health and vitality. However, calorie watchers should limit their consumption of starchy vegetables, such as beans and peas, because they have more calories than other vegetables.

Salads rate high with dieters because most of their ingredients are low calorie and versatile. You can combine crisp greens, other vegetables, fruits, and meat or fish in an endless variety of tempting dishes. Whatever your salad choice, avoid rich dressings. Instead keep several tangy low-calorie dressings on hand to avoid unwanted calories. Or try just a splash of lemon juice or red wine vinegar on salad greens for a low-calorie change of taste.

NUTRITIONAL ANALYSIS

Per Serving

	CALORIES	PROTEIN gms.	CARBOHYDRATE gms.	FAT gms.	SODIUM mgs.	POTASSIUM mgs.	PROTEIN	VITAMIN A	VITAMIN C	THIAMINE	RIBOFLAVIN	NIACIN	CALCIUM	IRON
VEGETABLES														
Caraway Brussels Sprouts (p. 69)	70	4	10	2	342	315	6	10	105	6	10	2	7	4
Cauliflower Casserole (p. 69)	58	3	6	3	444	230	5	4	69	3	7	4	7	4
Chilled Cucumber Soup (p. 68)	62	2	6	3	252	151	4	4	9	2	7	1	8	1
Corn Pudding (p. 69)	131	7	16	5	478	203	11	11	9	5	13	3	10	5
Creamy Broccoli Casserole (p. 68)	63	5	7	2	200	242	7	39	85	4	10	2	10	3
Herbed Green Beans (p. 68)	42	2	5	2	76	174	2	16	26	4	6	3	3	5
Italian Artichokes (p. 67)	21	2	7	0	180	233	3	6	13	4	2	3	3	5
Kohlrabi Soup (p. 68)	52	4	10	0	354	396	6	3	87	5	9	2	11	3
Lemon-Sesame Asparagus (p. 66)	56	2	5	4	171	251	4	18	49	10	10	7	2	5
Mushroom-Barley Casserole (p. 67)	144	3	23	5	332	121	5	9	15	3	4	6	1	5
Pineapple Carrots (p. 66)	60	1	14	0	185	406	2	240	21	6	4	4	5	5
Quick Ratatouille-Style Vegetables (p. 66)	46	2	6	2	101	266	2	16	70	5	4	5	2	4
Sautéed Mushrooms (p. 66)	51	2	4	3	108	254	3	7	9	4	15	11	1	3
Steamed Summer Squash (p. 67)	54	2	6	3	172	289	3	15	60	5	7	7	4	4
Steamed Vegetable Medley (p. 69)	60	2	5	4	240	235	3	43	51	4	6	4	2	4
Stir-Fried Vegetables (p. 67)	92	4	10	5	542	451	6	8	24	11	8	7	3	7
Stuffed Potatoes (p. 66)	70	3	13	1	563	308	5	2	24	5	5	5	6	3
Tangy Potato Topper (p. 66)	11	2	1	0	80	23	2	1	1	0	2	0	2	0

	Per Serving						Percent U.S. RDA Per Serving							
	CALORIES	PROTEIN gms.	CARBOHYDRATE gms.	FAT gms.	SODIUM mgs.	POTASSIUM mgs.	PROTEIN	VITAMIN A	VITAMIN C	THIAMINE	RIBOFLAVIN	NIACIN	CALCIUM	IRON
SALADS														
Apple and Cottage Cheese Slaw (p. 73)	137	13	12	5	216	229	19	5	30	4	17	1	13	3
Broccoli-Sprout Tossed Salad (p. 71)	71	2	5	5	9	222	3	13	59	5	8	4	3	4
Cabbage-Carrot Mold (p. 74)	70	2	3	6	298	106	2	41	21	1	1	1	2	1
Calorie Counter's Coleslaw (p. 73)	41	1	9	0	78	185	2	33	28	2	4	1	5	2
Cottage Cheese and Fruit Salad (p. 72)	114	4	26	0	55	304	6	8	49	8	6	2	5	4
Creamy Gelatin Salad (p. 72)	70	3	14	1	15	245	5	5	87	7	5	2	5	1
Creamy Salad Dressing (p. 75)	20	1	1	1	57	20	2	3	1	1	2	1	2	1
Crunchy Applesauce Mold (p. 73)	77	3	15	1	30	156	5	2	4	2	6	1	7	2
Cucumber-Cheese Mold (p. 72)	42	7	3	0	203	92	11	1	8	2	7	1	4	2
Diet Blue Cheese Dressing (p. 75)	13	1	1	1	15	21	1	0	0	0	2	0	2	0
Diet Salad Dressing (p. 75)	22	1	2	1	98	29	2	2	0	1	3	0	2	1
Diet Tartar Sauce (p. 75)	24	1	3	1	126	36	2	3	2	1	3	0	2	1
Diet Thousand Island Dressing (p. 75)	21	1	3	1	98	35	1	3	5	1	2	0	2	1
Dilled Cucumber Salad (p. 72)	34	3	4	1	108	142	5	4	13	2	5	1	5	4
Fruit Mold (p. 72)	90	3	20	1	32	258	5	2	13	4	6	2	7	2
Ginger Fruit Slaw (p. 74)	135	3	34	0	30	503	4	98	98	9	6	6	6	10
Ginger-Wine Vinaigrette (p. 75)	48	0	1	5	0	8	0	0	0	0	0	0	0	0
Herbed Tomatoes (p. 73)	138	2	7	12	361	350	3	29	58	6	4	5	3	5
Italian Salad Bowl (p. 71)	57	4	6	3	294	419	6	131	84	6	10	3	11	12
Marinated Tomato-Vegetable Salad (p. 71)	55	1	7	2	93	232	2	14	33	4	4	3	3	4
Marinated Vegetable Salad (p. 74)	93	2	15	4	536	208	2	118	11	3	3	3	6	10
Minted Fruit Cup (p. 73)	79	1	19	1	9	230	2	4	48	6	4	2	4	2
Molded Gazpacho Salad (p. 72)	30	3	6	0	332	280	4	17	48	4	2	3	2	6
Molded Strawberry Salads (p. 74)	62	3	12	1	18	139	4	1	49	2	5	2	5	3
Orange-Cucumber Salad (p. 74)	57	2	12	1	154	285	3	9	107	7	7	2	8	5
Orange Waldorf Salad (p. 71)	81	2	19	1	27	273	3	5	61	6	5	2	7	3
Spiced Fruit Salad (p. 71)	73	1	17	0	2	247	1	8	22	3	3	3	1	3
Tomato Salad Dressing (p. 75)	6	0	1	0	166	6	0	3	2	1	0	1	0	0
Wilted Spinach Salad (p. 71)	43	3	5	2	80	328	4	80	50	6	10	4	5	11

Side Dishes
Vegetables

Lemon-Sesame Asparagus
56/serving

  12 ounces fresh asparagus
       spears *or* one 8-ounce
       package frozen
       asparagus spears
   1 tablespoon butter *or* margarine
   2 teaspoons sesame seed
   2 teaspoons lemon juice

Wash and trim fresh asparagus. Cook, covered, in boiling salted water 10 to 15 minutes or till crisp-tender. (*Or*, cook frozen asparagus according to package directions.)

Meanwhile, in small saucepan heat and stir butter and sesame seed over low heat about 5 minutes or till seeds are golden brown. Add lemon juice and ¼ teaspoon *salt*. Drain asparagus; remove to heated serving dish. Pour lemon mixture over hot asparagus. Serve immediately. Serves 4.

Quick Ratatouille-Style Vegetables—46/serving

   1 small onion, sliced and
       separated into rings
   1 small clove garlic, minced
   2 teaspoons butter *or* margarine
   1 small green pepper, cut
       into strips
   1 medium zucchini, cut into
       ¼-inch slices
   1 7½-ounce can tomatoes,
       cut up
   ⅛ teaspoon dried oregano,
       crushed

In medium saucepan cook onion and garlic in butter till tender. Add green pepper, zucchini, *undrained* tomatoes, oregano, dash *salt*, and dash *pepper*. Bring to boiling; reduce heat. Simmer, uncovered, for 15 to 20 minutes or till all vegetables are tender. Serve immediately. Makes 4 servings.

Sautéed Mushrooms
51/serving

   3 cups sliced fresh mushrooms
       (8 ounces)
   ½ cup sliced green onion
   2 tablespoons dry white wine
   1 tablespoon butter *or* margarine
   ¼ teaspoon pepper
   ⅛ teaspoon salt

In skillet combine mushrooms, onion, wine, butter, pepper and salt. Cook over medium-high heat about 5 minutes or till mushrooms are lightly browned and some of the liquid has evaporated. Serve immediately. Makes 4 servings.

Pineapple Carrots
60/serving
pictured on pages 62 and 63

   ½ of an 8-ounce can crushed
       pineapple (juice pack)
   ½ cup water
   ¼ teaspoon salt
   4 large carrots, cut into
       julienne strips (2 cups)
   1 teaspoon cornstarch
   1 tablespoon snipped parsley

Drain pineapple, reserving 2 tablespoons juice. In saucepan combine drained crushed pineapple, the water, and salt. Add carrots. Cover and simmer 12 to 15 minutes or till tender. Combine the reserved pineapple juice and the cornstarch. Add to carrots; cook and stir over low heat till bubbly. Stir in the snipped parsley. Season to taste with salt and pepper. Makes 4 servings.

Tangy Potato Topper

Baked potatoes aren't fattening until you pile on the butter and sour cream. Then the calories really mount up! For a nutritious topping substitute, try this low-calorie creamy alternative.

In blender container combine ½ cup *dry cottage cheese*; 3 tablespoons *skim milk*; ¼ teaspoon *salt*; ¼ teaspoon dried *basil*, crushed; ¼ teaspoon *onion powder*; and dash *pepper*. Cover and blend till smooth. Stir in ¼ cup *plain yogurt* and 1 tablespoon snipped *parsley*. Serve over baked potatoes. Makes ⅔ cup. (11/tablespoon).

Stuffed Potatoes—70/serving
pictured on pages 62 and 63

   2 large potatoes
   ¼ cup plain yogurt
   1 tablespoon skim milk
   2 tablespoons snipped chives
   1 teaspoon salt
   ⅛ teaspoon garlic powder
       Dash pepper
   2 tablespoons grated Parmesan
       cheese
       Paprika

Scrub potatoes; prick with a fork. Bake potatoes in a 375° oven for 70 minutes or till done. Slice potatoes in half lengthwise. Scoop out inside, leaving shells intact. Mash potatoes. Add yogurt, milk, chives, salt, garlic powder, and pepper. Beat till fluffy. Spoon or pipe the potato mixture into each potato shell. Sprinkle the top of each potato with cheese and paprika. Return to oven; bake 10 minutes or till heated through. If desired, place under broiler to lightly brown tops. Makes 4 servings.

Italian Artichokes
21/serving

- 2 pounds fresh tiny artichokes *or* medium artichokes, quartered
  Lemon juice
- 1¾ cups water
- 2 tablespoons tomato paste
- 2 teaspoons instant chicken bouillon granules
- ½ teaspoon dried tarragon, crushed

Wash, trim stems, and remove loose outer leaves from artichokes. If using quartered medium artichokes, scoop out choke and discard. Cut off 1 inch of tops; snip off sharp leaf tips. Brush cut edges with lemon juice. In 10-inch skillet combine water, tomato paste, instant chicken bouillon granules, and tarragon. Bring to boiling. Reduce heat; add artichokes. Cover and simmer for 18 to 20 minutes or till a leaf pulls out of artichoke easily; stir occasionally. Remove artichokes with slotted spoon. Pour sauce into individual bowls for dipping. Makes 6 servings.

Mushroom-Barley Casserole
144/serving

- ⅔ cup quick-cooking barley
- ¼ cup chopped onion
- 2 tablespoons butter *or* margarine
- 1 4-ounce can mushroom stems and pieces
- 1¾ cups water
- 2 tablespoons chopped pimiento
- 2 tablespoons snipped parsley
- 2 teaspoons instant chicken bouillon granules
- ¼ teaspoon dried rosemary, crushed

In small skillet cook barley and onion in butter or margarine till barley is lightly browned and onion is tender. Drain mushrooms, reserving 3 tablespoons liquid. Add mushrooms and reserved liquid, water, pimiento, parsley, instant chicken bouillon granules, and rosemary to skillet; stir to combine ingredients.

Turn into a 1-quart casserole. Cover and bake in 350° oven for 1 hour or till barley is tender. Uncover and bake 10 minutes more or till liquid is absorbed. Makes 5 servings.

Steamed Summer Squash
54/serving

- 6 small zucchini (1¼ pounds)
- 4 small yellow crookneck squash (1 pound)
- ½ cup thinly sliced onion
- 2 tablespoons butter *or* margarine
- 1 tablespoon lemon juice
- ½ teaspoon salt
- ½ teaspoon dried basil, crushed
- ⅛ teaspoon pepper
- 1 2-ounce can sliced pimiento, drained and chopped

Cut zucchini and crookneck squash into ½-inch-thick slices. Place sliced zucchini and yellow squash and sliced onion in steamer basket. Place basket over boiling water. Cover and steam about 13 minutes or till vegetables are tender.

Meanwhile, in saucepan melt butter or margarine. Stir in lemon juice, salt, basil, and pepper. Turn steamed vegetables into serving bowl. Stir in butter mixture and pimiento. Serve immediately. Makes 8 servings.

Stir-Fried Vegetables
92/serving

Keep the food moving constantly so all the ingredients are cooked as quickly and evenly as possible—

- ½ teaspoon instant beef bouillon granules
- ¼ cup boiling water
- 2 teaspoons cornstarch
  Dash crushed red pepper *or* cayenne
- 2 tablespoons soy sauce
- 2 tablespoons cooking oil
- 1 medium onion, sliced and separated into rings
- 1 cup bias-sliced celery *or* bok choy
- 1 clove garlic, minced
- 1 cup sliced fresh mushrooms
- 1 8-ounce can bamboo shoots, drained
- 1 cup fresh pea pods *or* one 6-ounce package frozen pea pods, thawed
- 1 medium tomato, cut into wedges

Dissolve beef bouillon granules in boiling water. Stir together cornstarch, red pepper or cayenne, and soy sauce. Stir in beef bouillon mixture; set aside.

Preheat a wok or large skillet over high heat; add cooking oil. Stir-fry onion rings, sliced celery or bok choy, and minced garlic in hot oil for 1 to 2 minutes. Remove vegetables from wok or skillet. Add mushrooms and bamboo shoots to wok or skillet. Stir-fry 2 minutes.

Stir bouillon-soy mixture; stir into mushroom mixture. Cook and stir till bubbly. Stir in onion-celery mixture, pea pods, and tomato wedges. Cover and cook 1 minute. Serve immediately. Makes 6 servings.

Side Dishes
Vegetables

Vegetable Dress-Ups

To add that special touch to your vegetable cookery, dress up plain vegetables with these simple and low-calorie additions. Add crunch to cooked vegetables with sliced celery or green pepper. For a touch of tartness, add a teaspoon of lemon juice or a little plain yogurt. For color contrast, add chopped pimiento, sliced hard-cooked eggs, shredded carrot, or snipped chives or parsley.

Creamy Broccoli Casserole
63/serving

- 1 10-ounce package frozen cut broccoli
- ¼ cup chopped onion
- ½ cup *reconstituted* nonfat dry milk
- 1½ teaspoons cornstarch
- ¼ teaspoon salt
- ¼ teaspoon dried thyme, crushed
- 1 ounce Neufchâtel cheese
- 1 tablespoon grated Parmesan cheese

Cook frozen broccoli according to package directions. Drain, reserving cooking liquid. Cook onion in reserved cooking liquid for 5 minutes or till tender. *Do not drain.* In screw-top jar combine milk, cornstarch, salt, thyme, and dash *pepper*. Stir into onion. Cook and stir till bubbly. Stir in Neufchâtel cheese. Add broccoli. Gently stir to mix. Turn into serving bowl. Sprinkle Parmesan atop. Serves 4.

Herbed Green Beans
42/serving

- 1 9-ounce package frozen cut *or* whole green beans
- ¼ cup sliced green onion
- 2 teaspoons butter *or* margarine
- 1 2-ounce can mushroom stems and pieces, drained
- 2 tablespoons chopped pimiento
- ¼ teaspoon dried marjoram, crushed
- ¼ teaspoon dried basil, crushed
  Dash salt
  Dash pepper

In saucepan cook frozen green beans according to package directions; drain well. In another saucepan cook onion in butter or margarine till tender. Stir in mushrooms, chopped pimiento, marjoram, basil, salt, and pepper. Stir in well-drained beans. Toss to coat; heat through. Transfer to serving bowl. Serve immediately. Makes 4 servings.

Kohlrabi Soup—52/serving

- 4 medium kohlrabi, peeled and sliced (2 cups)
- ½ cup chopped onion
- 1½ teaspoons instant chicken bouillon granules
- 1 cup skim milk
- ¼ teaspoon salt
  Dash white pepper
  Snipped chives *or* parsley

In saucepan combine kohlrabi, onion, bouillon granules, and 1 cup *water*. Bring to boiling; reduce heat. Cover; simmer about 20 minutes or till kohlrabi is tender. Pour mixture into blender container; cover and blend till smooth. Return mixture to saucepan. Stir in milk, salt, and pepper; heat through. To serve, ladle into bowls; top with chives. Makes 4 servings.

Versatile Cucumbers

Take advantage of a cucumber's bountiful uses: Slice it for a refreshing and nutritious snack. Add it to tossed salads, molded salads, and relish trays. Combine it with onion slices in a vinegar dressing.

To keep cucumber slices crisp, cut them very thin and place immediately in ice water. Refrigerate.

Chilled Cucumber Soup
62/serving

- 1 medium cucumber, peeled, seeded, and chopped (1 cup)
- 2 tablespoons sliced green onion
- 1 tablespoon butter *or* margarine
- 2 teaspoons cornstarch
- ¾ cup water
- ½ cup *reconstituted* nonfat dry milk
- 1 teaspoon instant chicken bouillon granules
- ¼ teaspoon dried dillweed
- ⅛ teaspoon salt
- ½ cup plain yogurt
  Sliced green onion tops

In saucepan cook cucumber and onion in butter or margarine about 5 minutes or till tender. Stir in cornstarch. Add water, milk, bouillon granules, dillweed, and salt. Cook and stir till slightly thickened and bubbly. Cook and stir 2 minutes more. Pour mixture into blender container; cover and blend till smooth. Stir cucumber mixture into yogurt. Cover and chill. Garnish with sliced green onion tops. Makes 4 servings.

Corn Pudding—131/serving

- ⅓ cup chopped onion
- 2 teaspoons butter *or* margarine
- 1 cup skim milk
- ½ teaspoon salt
- ⅛ teaspoon pepper
- 2 beaten eggs
- 1 8-ounce can whole kernel corn, drained

Cook onion in butter or margarine till tender but not brown. Stir in milk, salt, and pepper; heat almost to boiling. Gradually stir milk mixture into beaten eggs; add corn. Turn into four 6-ounce custard cups. Place in 8x8x2-inch baking pan; pour hot water into pan around custard cups to depth of 1 inch. Bake in 350° oven for 20 to 25 minutes or till knife inserted near center comes out clean. Makes 4 servings.

Cauliflower Casserole 58/serving

- 2 10-ounce packages frozen cauliflower
- 1 10¾-ounce can condensed cream of celery soup
- 1 4-ounce can mushroom stems and pieces, drained
- ¼ cup sliced green onion
- ½ teaspoon dried basil, crushed
- ¼ teaspoon salt
  Dash pepper
- ¼ cup grated Parmesan cheese
- ½ teaspoon paprika

Cook cauliflower according to package directions; drain well. Halve any large pieces. In 2-quart casserole combine soup, mushrooms, onion, basil, salt, and pepper. Carefully stir in cauliflower. Sprinkle Parmesan cheese and paprika atop. Bake, uncovered, in a 375° oven for 25 minutes or till heated through. Makes 8 servings.

Caraway Brussels Sprouts 70/serving

- 1 10-ounce package frozen brussels sprouts
- ¼ cup chopped onion
- 2 teaspoons butter *or* margarine
- ½ cup skim milk
- 2 teaspoons cornstarch
- 1 teaspoon caraway seed
- 1 teaspoon Worcestershire sauce
- ¼ cup plain yogurt

Cook brussels sprouts according to package directions; drain. Cook onion in butter or margarine till tender. In screw-top jar combine milk, cornstarch, caraway, Worcestershire, ½ teaspoon *salt*, and dash *pepper*; shake well. Add to onion. Cook and stir till thickened and bubbly. Stir in yogurt. Stir well-drained brussels sprouts into sauce; heat through. Serves 4.

Steamed Vegetable Medley 60/serving

- 2 cups cauliflower flowerets
- 1 cup bias-sliced carrots
- 1 medium red onion, sliced and separated into rings
- 1 cup whole fresh mushrooms
- 2 tablespoons butter
- 1 tablespoon lemon juice
- ½ teaspoon salt
- ¼ teaspoon dried dillweed

Place cauliflower, carrots, and onion in steamer basket. Place basket over boiling water. Cover and steam for 15 minutes. Halve any large mushrooms. Add mushrooms; cover and steam for 5 minutes more or till all vegetables are tender.

Meanwhile, in saucepan melt butter. Add lemon juice, salt, dillweed, and ⅛ teaspoon *pepper*. To serve, transfer vegetables to serving bowl. Pour lemon mixture over vegetables; toss to coat. Serves 6.

Steaming Fresh Vegetables

Steam cooking your vegetables ensures their optimum natural freshness and flavor because steamed foods retain their shape, texture, and nutrients.

It is easy to steam cook fresh vegetables if you follow these simple steps and timings. Prepare the fresh vegetables by thoroughly rinsing them in cool water. Depending upon the type of vegetable, trim stems, remove outer leaves, or peel. Place vegetable in steamer basket (see note below); place over, but not touching, boiling water. Cover; reduce heat. Steam following timings below or till desired doneness. Drain; season to taste. If a combination of vegetables is desired, start with the longest cooking vegetable; add others at appropriate time.

Asparagus, cut up	13 minutes
Beans, cut into ½-inch pieces	23 minutes
Broccoli, spears	20 minutes
cut up	16 minutes
Brussels sprouts	20 minutes
Cabbage, wedges	15 minutes
Carrots	23 minutes
Cauliflower, flowerets	15 minutes
Onions, quartered	25 minutes
Squash, summer, cut into ¼-inch slices	13 minutes
Squash, winter, cut into ¼-inch slices	18 minutes

Note: If you don't own a metal steamer basket, you can improvise with a metal can and rack. Simply remove the top and bottom of a metal can (about 3 inches tall and 4 inches wide); place it in a large saucepan. Place a wire rack on top of the can. Add water to just below rack; bring to boiling. Position food in a heat-proof serving dish atop the wire rack. Cover; cook just till food is done.

Broccoli-Sprout Tossed Salad—71/serving

    5 cups torn salad greens
    1 cup fresh broccoli buds
    1 cup fresh bean sprouts
    1 cup sliced fresh mushrooms
    1 medium red onion, sliced
        and separated into rings
    ½ cup green pepper strips
    ½ cup Ginger-Wine Vinaigrette
        (see recipe, page 75)

In salad bowl combine torn salad greens, broccoli buds, bean sprouts, sliced mushrooms, onion rings, and green pepper strips. Pass Ginger-Wine Vinaigrette to drizzle over all. Makes 8 servings.

Orange Waldorf Salad 81/serving

    3 medium oranges, peeled and
        sectioned
    1½ cups chopped apple
    ½ cup chopped celery
    ½ cup lemon yogurt
    2 teaspoons honey
      Dash salt
      Lettuce

Cut up orange sections over bowl, reserving juice. Toss oranges and juice with apple and celery. Chill. Combine yogurt, honey, and salt; fold into fruit mixture. Spoon about ½ cup onto each of 6 lettuce-lined salad plates. Makes 6 servings.

Tangy *Ginger-Wine Vinaigrette* (see recipe, page 75) complements fresh *Broccoli-Sprout Tossed Salad.*

Wilted Spinach Salad 43/serving

    8 cups spinach leaves
    1 cup sliced fresh mushrooms
    1 slice bacon
    2 tablespoons finely chopped
        onion
    2 tablespoons vinegar
    1 tablespoon catsup
    1 tablespoon water
    1 teaspoon sugar
    ¼ teaspoon dried marjoram,
        crushed
    ½ cup alfalfa sprouts

Tear spinach leaves into bite-size pieces and place in a bowl; add mushrooms. Cut up bacon. In a deep 10-inch skillet cook bacon pieces till crisp; *do not drain.* Add onion, vinegar, catsup, water, sugar, and marjoram. Stir till bubbly. Remove skillet from heat. Stir spinach mixture into skillet, tossing till all the greens are slightly wilted and well coated. Turn salad into serving bowl; sprinkle alfalfa sprouts atop and toss. Makes 8 servings.

Spiced Fruit Salad 73/serving

    1 8-ounce can peach slices
    ¼ cup orange juice
    2 tablespoons dry white wine
    ¼ teaspoon ground cinnamon
      Dash ground nutmeg
    1 medium apple, cored and
        sliced
    1 small banana, sliced

In mixing bowl combine *undrained* peach slices, orange juice, white wine, cinnamon, and nutmeg. Stir in apple and banana slices. Cover and chill for 1 hour. Serve in individual bowls. Makes 4 servings.

Marinated Tomato-Vegetable Salad—55/serving

pictured on pages 62 and 63

    ½ of a 9-ounce package frozen
        cut green beans *or* one
        8-ounce can cut green
        beans
    2 medium tomatoes, cut into
        wedges
    1 small onion, thinly sliced and
        separated into rings
    1 medium zucchini, sliced
    3 tablespoons snipped parsley
    ⅓ cup vinegar
    2 tablespoons rosé wine
    1 tablespoon salad oil
    2 teaspoons sugar
    ¼ teaspoon dried basil, crushed

Cook frozen green beans according to package directions; drain. (*Or,* drain canned beans.) In bowl combine green beans, tomatoes, onion rings, zucchini slices, and parsley.

In screw-top jar combine vinegar, rosé wine, oil, sugar, basil, and ¼ teaspoon *salt.* Cover; shake well. Pour over vegetables in bowl. Cover; refrigerate several hours or overnight, stirring occasionally. Drain to serve. Serve on lettuce-lined salad plates, if desired. Serves 6.

Italian Salad Bowl 57/serving

    6 cups torn spinach leaves
    1 cup sliced radishes
    1 small green pepper, cut into
        strips
    1 cup shredded carrot
    ¼ cup grated Parmesan cheese
    ⅔ cup low-calorie Italian
        salad dressing

In salad bowl combine spinach, radishes, green pepper, shredded carrot, and Parmesan cheese. Toss to mix. Cover and chill, if desired. Pour dressing over salad. Toss to coat. Makes 6 servings.

Side Dishes
Salads

Fruit Mold—90/serving

1   envelope unflavored gelatin
½   cup cold water
1   teaspoon sugar
1   tablespoon lemon juice
1   cup lemon yogurt
1   8-ounce can crushed pineapple
        (juice pack)
2   small bananas, thinly sliced
        (1 cup)
⅓   cup chopped celery
    Lettuce

In saucepan soften gelatin in cold water; stir in sugar. Stir over low heat till gelatin and sugar are dissolved. Cool. Add lemon juice. Beat lemon yogurt into cooled mixture till smooth. Stir in *undrained* pineapple, bananas, and celery. Pour into 3-cup mold; chill till firm. Unmold onto lettuce-lined plate. Makes 6 servings.

Cucumber-Cheese Mold 42/serving

1   envelope unflavored gelatin
1¼ cups cold water
1½ teaspoons instant chicken
        bouillon granules
2   teaspoons lemon juice
1   teaspoon prepared
        horseradish
1½ cups dry cottage cheese
1   large cucumber, peeled,
        seeded, and shredded
2   tablespoons chopped
        green onion
    Lettuce

In small saucepan soften gelatin in water; add bouillon granules. Stir over low heat till gelatin is dissolved; cool. Stir in lemon juice and horseradish. Add cottage cheese, shredded cucumber, and chopped green onion. Turn into a 4-cup mold. Chill till firm. Unmold onto lettuce-lined plate; garnish with cucumber slices, if desired. Makes 8 servings.

Creamy Gelatin Salad 70/serving

2   envelopes unflavored gelatin
1   cup cold orange juice
2¼ cups orange juice
1   medium orange, peeled,
        sectioned, and chopped
1   cup plain yogurt
1   tablespoon sugar

Soften gelatin in the 1 cup cold orange juice. In medium saucepan heat *1¾ cups* of the orange juice just to boiling. Add the softened gelatin; stir to dissolve. Set aside *1 cup* of the gelatin mixture and keep at room temperature.

Stir remaining ½ cup orange juice into remaining gelatin mixture. Chill till partially set. Add the cut-up orange sections. Pour into an 8x8x2-inch pan; chill till almost firm. Combine yogurt and sugar; beat in reserved gelatin. Spoon over fruit layer. Chill till firm. Serves 9.

Cottage Cheese and Fruit Salad—114/serving

1   11-ounce can mandarin orange
        sections, chilled
1   8-ounce can pineapple chunks
        (juice pack), chilled
½   cup dry cottage cheese
1   medium banana
1   medium apple
    Lemon juice
    Lettuce

Drain orange sections and pineapple chunks; reserve ¼ cup of the fruit liquid. In blender container combine cottage cheese and reserved fruit liquid. Cover; blend till smooth. Slice banana. Core and chop apple. Dip banana slices and chopped apple into a little lemon juice. Combine all fruits; spoon onto lettuce-lined salad plates. Dollop cottage cheese mixture atop. Makes 4 servings.

Molded Gazpacho Salad 30/serving

1   envelope unflavored gelatin
1   12-ounce can (1½ cups)
        vegetable juice cocktail
1   teaspoon instant beef
        bouillon granules
¼   cup water
½   teaspoon Worcestershire
        sauce
    Few drops bottled hot pepper
        sauce
½   cup finely chopped celery
¼   cup finely chopped green
        pepper
2   tablespoons sliced green
        onion

In saucepan soften gelatin in vegetable juice cocktail; add bouillon granules. Stir over low heat till gelatin is dissolved. Remove from heat. Stir in water, Worcestershire sauce, and hot pepper sauce. Chill till partially set. Fold in chopped celery, chopped green pepper, and sliced green onion. Turn into 4 individual molds or one 2½-cup mold. Chill till firm. Unmold to serve. Makes 4 servings.

Dilled Cucumber Salad 34/serving

½   cup cream-style cottage
        cheese
½   cup plain yogurt
¼   teaspoon dried dillweed
¼   teaspoon salt
2   medium cucumbers, thinly
        sliced
1   medium onion, thinly sliced

In blender container combine cottage cheese, yogurt, dillweed, and salt. Cover and blend till smooth. In bowl combine cucumber and onion. Stir in yogurt mixture. Cover and chill. Makes 8 servings.

Calorie Counter's Coleslaw
41/serving

  2   cups shredded cabbage
  ¾   cup shredded carrot
  ½   cup thinly sliced celery
  2   tablespoons sliced green
        onion
  ½   cup plain yogurt
  2   teaspoons sugar
  1   teaspoon prepared
        horseradish
  ⅛   teaspoon salt
        Dash pepper

In salad bowl toss together shredded cabbage, shredded carrot, sliced celery, and sliced green onion. For dressing, stir together plain yogurt, sugar, horseradish, salt, and pepper. Toss dressing with cabbage mixture till all ingredients are well-coated. Cover; chill several hours. Makes 6 servings.

Minted Fruit Cup
79/serving

  ½   cup plain yogurt
  2   tablespoons lime juice
  2 or 3 teaspoons snipped fresh
        mint
  2   cups seedless green or red
        grapes, halved
  3   medium oranges, peeled and
        sectioned
  2   medium apples, cored and
        sliced

Stir together plain yogurt, lime juice, and mint. Combine halved grapes, orange sections, and sliced apples. Pour yogurt mixture over fruit; toss to coat. Cover and chill. To serve, spoon fruit into 8 individual serving dishes. Makes 8 servings.

Unmolding a Gelatin Salad

Tower or ring gelatin salads aren't that tricky to unmold—they just seem it.

To begin, dip the mold just to the rim in warm water for a *few seconds*. Tilt slightly to ease gelatin away from one side and let air in. With the tip of a small metal spatula, loosen the gelatin from mold by carefully running the spatula around the edges. Place hand over the gelatin and tilt or rotate the mold to let air loosen the gelatin all the way around the salad. Invert mold onto lettuce-lined plate; shake the mold gently. Lift off the mold, being careful not to tear the gelatin. Garnish.

Crunchy Applesauce Mold
77/serving

  1   envelope unflavored gelatin
  ¾   cup cold water
  1   cup lemon yogurt
  ½   cup unsweetened applesauce
  ⅛   teaspoon ground cinnamon
  1   cup finely chopped apple
        Lettuce

In saucepan soften gelatin in cold water; stir over low heat till dissolved. In bowl combine lemon yogurt, applesauce, and cinnamon; stir in gelatin. Chill till partially set. Fold in chopped apple. Turn into 3-cup mold. Chill till firm. To serve, unmold onto lettuce-lined plate. Makes 5 servings.

Herbed Tomatoes
138/serving

  6   medium tomatoes
  ⅔   cup salad oil
  ¼   cup snipped parsley
  ¼   cup sliced green onion
  ¼   cup wine vinegar
  2   teaspoons snipped fresh
        marjoram or ½ teaspoon
        dried marjoram, crushed
  1   teaspoon salt
  ¼   teaspoon pepper
        Lettuce

Peel and quarter tomatoes; place in a deep bowl. In a screw-top jar combine oil, parsley, green onion, vinegar, marjoram, salt, and pepper; shake well. Pour over tomatoes. Cover and refrigerate several hours or overnight, spooning herb mixture over tomatoes occasionally. At serving time, lift tomatoes from marinade with slotted spoon. Serve on lettuce-lined platter. Spoon some of the herb mixture over tomatoes again. Makes 6 servings.

Apple and Cottage Cheese Slaw—137/serving

  2   cups shredded cabbage
  1   medium apple, cored and
        diced
  ½   cup Diet Blue Cheese Dressing
        (see recipe, page 75)
  1½ cups cream-style cottage
        cheese (12 ounces)

In salad bowl combine shredded cabbage and diced apple. Pour Diet Blue Cheese Dressing over cabbage mixture; toss to coat. Spoon cottage cheese in ring atop cabbage mixture. Makes 4 servings.

Salads

Molded Strawberry Salads
62/serving

- 2 cups frozen whole unsweetened strawberries
- 1 envelope unflavored gelatin
- 1 cup water
- ¾ cup lemon yogurt
- 1 tablespoon honey

Thaw strawberries. Press 1 cup of the berries through a fine-meshed sieve with the back of a wooden spoon. Slice remaining berries. Soften gelatin in water; heat to dissolve gelatin. Stir in the mashed berries, lemon yogurt, and honey. Chill till partially set. Fold in the sliced strawberries. Turn mixture into a 3-cup mold. Chill till firm. Unmold onto serving platter. Makes 6 servings.

Orange-Cucumber Salad
57/serving

- ½ of a large cucumber, thinly sliced (1 cup)
- ¼ teaspoon salt
  Dash pepper
- 2 medium oranges, peeled and sectioned
- ½ cup chopped green pepper
- 2 tablespoons snipped parsley
- ½ cup plain yogurt
- ¼ teaspoon dried thyme, crushed
  Torn salad greens (optional)

In mixing bowl sprinkle cucumber with the salt and pepper; toss with orange sections, green pepper, and parsley. Combine yogurt and thyme; spoon onto salad mixture. Toss lightly to coat. Cover and chill. Serve on crisp salad greens, if desired. Makes 4 servings.

Cabbage-Carrot Mold
70/serving

- 1 envelope unflavored gelatin
- 1 cup boiling water
- 1 teaspoon instant chicken bouillon granules
- ¼ cup creamy Italian salad dressing
- ¼ teaspoon dried dillweed
- 1 cup finely shredded cabbage
- 1 cup finely shredded carrot
- 2 tablespoons finely chopped green pepper
  Lettuce

Soften gelatin in ½ cup cold *water*. Add 1 cup boiling water and chicken bouillon granules; heat and stir till gelatin is dissolved. Remove from heat. Stir in salad dressing and dillweed. Chill till partially set. Fold in cabbage, carrot, and green pepper. Turn mixture into a 3-cup mold. Cover and chill several hours or overnight till firm. Unmold onto lettuce-lined plate. Makes 6 servings.

Marinated Vegetable Salad
93/serving

- 1 16-ounce can cut green beans, drained
- 1 16-ounce can cut wax beans, drained
- 1 16-ounce can diced carrots, drained
- ½ cup chopped celery
- ⅓ cup vinegar
- ¼ cup sugar
- 2 tablespoons salad oil
- ½ teaspoon salt

In mixing bowl combine green beans, wax beans, carrots, and celery. Combine vinegar, sugar, salad oil, salt, and ⅛ teaspoon *pepper*; pour over vegetables. Toss. Cover and chill several hours or overnight, stirring occasionally to distribute marinade. Drain to serve. Makes 8 servings.

Shredding Cabbage

Save time by shredding cabbage in the blender. Begin by removing and discarding any wilted outer leaves; rinse cabbage. Cut into wedges; remove center core. Then, fill blender container no more than half full with cabbage wedges; cover with cold water. Blend till chopped to desired coarseness. Remove from blender container; drain well. Repeat with remaining cabbage wedges. Cover and chill. Before serving, drain cabbage again. (Or, drain and use as directed in recipes for coleslaw and other similar dishes.)

Ginger Fruit Slaw
135/serving

- 1 8-ounce can crushed pineapple (juice pack)
- 5 cups shredded red cabbage (about 6 ounces)
- 3 large oranges, peeled and sectioned
- 2 large carrots, shredded
- ¾ cup snipped dried apricots
- ¼ cup honey
- 1 tablespoon lemon juice
- ½ teaspoon ground ginger

Drain pineapple, reserving ¼ cup of the juice; set aside. In a large bowl combine cabbage, orange sections, shredded carrots, snipped apricots, and crushed pineapple; cover and chill. In a screw-top jar combine reserved pineapple juice, honey, lemon juice, and ginger. Cover and chill. Just before serving, shake dressing; pour over cabbage mixture. Toss to mix. Makes 8 servings.

Tomato Salad Dressing
6/tablespoon

This zesty salad dressing is pictured on pages 62 and 63—

    1 8-ounce can tomato sauce
    2 tablespoons tarragon vinegar
    1 teaspoon Worcestershire
        sauce
    ½ teaspoon salt
    ½ teaspoon dried dillweed
    ½ teaspoon dried basil, crushed
    ½ teaspoon onion juice

In a screw-top jar combine the tomato sauce, tarragon vinegar, Worcestershire sauce, salt, dried dillweed, basil, and onion juice. Cover and shake well; chill thoroughly. Shake again before serving. Makes about 1 cup dressing.

Diet Thousand Island Dressing—21/tablespoon

This also makes a delicious spread on an open-faced sandwich —

    ½ cup Diet Salad Dressing
    1 tablespoon chopped green
        onion
    1 tablespoon chopped green
        pepper
    1 tablespoon catsup or chili
        sauce
    1 tablespoon chopped pimiento
    1 teaspoon prepared
        horseradish

In small mixing bowl stir together the Diet Salad Dressing, chopped green onion, chopped green pepper, catsup or chili sauce, chopped pimiento, and horseradish till well combined. Transfer to jar; cover tightly and chill. Makes ⅔ cup.

Diet Tartar Sauce
24/tablespoon

    ½ cup Diet Salad Dressing
    2 tablespoons finely chopped
        dill pickle
    1 tablespoon snipped parsley
    1 tablespoon chopped green
        onion

In bowl combine the Diet Salad Dressing, chopped pickle, snipped parsley, and green onion. Transfer to jar; cover and chill. Serve with fish. Makes ½ cup sauce.

Ginger-Wine Vinaigrette
48/tablespoon

pictured on page 70

    ½ cup red wine vinegar
    6 tablespoons salad oil
    2 teaspoons sugar
    1 teaspoon grated gingerroot or
        ½ teaspoon ground ginger
    1 teaspoon celery seed

In a screw-top jar combine wine vinegar, oil, sugar, gingerroot or ground ginger, and celery seed. Cover tightly; shake well. Chill. Makes 1 cup.

Diet Blue Cheese Dressing
13/tablespoon

    1 cup plain yogurt
    2 tablespoons crumbled blue
        cheese
    2 teaspoons sugar
    ½ teaspoon celery seed
        Dash bottled hot pepper sauce

In a small mixer bowl combine the plain yogurt, *1 tablespoon* of the crumbled blue cheese, the sugar, celery seed, and the bottled hot pepper sauce. Thoroughly beat dressing with rotary beater till smooth. Stir in the remaining crumbled blue cheese. Transfer to jar; cover tightly and chill. Makes about 1 cup.

Diet Salad Dressing
22/tablespoon

    1 tablespoon all-purpose flour
    1 tablespoon sugar
    1 teaspoon dry mustard
    ½ teaspoon salt
        Dash cayenne
    ¾ cup skim milk
    2 slightly beaten egg yolks
    3 tablespoons vinegar

In a saucepan combine the flour, sugar, dry mustard, salt, and cayenne; stir in the milk. Cook and stir till mixture is thickened and bubbly. Gradually stir some of the hot mixture into the slightly beaten egg yolks. Return all to saucepan. Cook, stirring constantly, 2 minutes more. Place a piece of waxed paper over the surface; cool 10 to 15 minutes. Remove waxed paper; stir in the vinegar. Transfer to jar; cover tightly and chill. Makes ¾ cup dressing.

Creamy Salad Dressing
20/tablespoon

    2 hard-cooked egg yolks
    1 raw egg yolk
    ½ cup plain yogurt
    2 teaspoons finely chopped
        onion
    1 teaspoon lemon juice
    1 teaspoon Dijon-style mustard
    ¼ teaspoon salt

Sieve hard-cooked egg yolks into small bowl. Blend in raw egg yolk. Stir in yogurt, onion, lemon juice, mustard, salt, and dash *pepper*. Mix well. Cover and chill. (Use within several days.) Makes ¾ cup.

Calorie-Trimmed
Desserts

Discover luscious desserts that are low-calorie, too! Pictured (from left): *Ambrosia Cream Puffs*, *Chocolate Angel Cake*, *Lime Freeze* with a lemon variation, and *Apricot Spanish Cream*. (See index for recipe pages.)

Desserts

If you have a sweet tooth (and who doesn't), then high-calorie desserts probably pose a very big obstacle to a successful diet. Just a few extra bites of a rich dessert can quickly add up to unwanted pounds. And when you are on a diet, those extra bites can lead to guilt feelings and even to your giving up completely calorie counting and weight control.

For the sweets-lover's dilemma we have the answers: delicious substitutes for old favorites. You can enjoy these substitutes and still watch your weight. With moderation and the low-calorie goodies in this chapter, you can have your cake and eat it, too. And that little sweet touch at the end of a meal may be just the boost you need for successful dieting.

NUTRITIONAL ANALYSIS

Per Serving | **Percent U.S. RDA Per Serving**

	CALORIES	PROTEIN gms.	CARBOHYDRATE gms.	FAT gms.	SODIUM mgs.	POTASSIUM mgs.	PROTEIN	VITAMIN A	VITAMIN C	THIAMINE	RIBOFLAVIN	NIACIN	CALCIUM	IRON
Ambrosia Cream Puffs (p. 79)	131	4	18	5	103	157	6	7	16	6	8	3	5	4
Apricot Spanish Cream (p. 84)	105	5	18	2	42	267	8	32	6	3	8	2	7	3
Berry-Rice Pudding (p. 83)	108	4	17	3	114	149	6	3	31	4	9	2	7	3
Chocolate Angel Cake (p. 79)	96	3	21	0	64	53	5	0	0	4	5	2	1	2
Chocolate Bavarian (p. 84)	87	4	12	3	67	114	7	4	1	2	8	0	7	2
Choco-Mint Roll (p. 82)	125	4	21	3	111	96	7	6	0	2	7	1	5	4
Citrus-Cheese Sauce (p. 82)	16	1	2	1	18	18	1	1	1	0	1	0	1	0
Coffee Meringues (p. 82)	107	2	18	3	25	33	3	4	0	1	4	0	2	2
Cream Puffs (p. 79)	74	2	6	4	82	24	4	5	0	4	4	2	1	3
Lemon Pudding Cake (p. 81)	109	4	14	4	72	94	6	6	6	3	8	1	6	2
Lemon Soufflé (p. 83)	102	5	11	4	48	95	8	5	8	2	8	0	6	2
Lime Freeze (p. 85)	74	3	11	3	33	72	4	4	5	1	6	0	5	1
Maple Dessert Cups (p. 85)	66	3	8	3	36	95	4	2	0	1	5	0	6	1
Orange Cake Roll (p. 81)	135	4	22	3	113	73	5	6	17	5	6	2	2	3
Peach Dessert Sauce (p. 85)	47	1	10	0	18	86	2	4	2	1	4	1	5	0
Pineapple Fluff (p. 85)	97	4	14	3	46	148	7	6	8	5	9	1	6	4
Polynesian Parfaits (p. 81)	100	2	24	1	17	294	3	7	47	8	6	2	7	3
Rum-Custard Soufflé (p. 84)	88	5	11	3	118	105	8	6	1	2	9	0	7	3
Steamed Cranberry Pudding (p. 83)	137	2	30	1	142	174	3	0	3	8	4	4	3	7
Stirred Custard (p. 82)	112	7	12	4	88	181	11	7	2	4	16	0	13	4
Strawberry Sponge Cake (p. 79)	120	3	21	3	26	101	5	4	37	2	6	1	3	4
Wine Fruit Medley (p. 81)	72	1	16	0	2	229	1	7	45	3	3	3	1	3
Yogurt-Sauced Peaches (p. 84)	87	3	18	1	44	316	5	36	16	3	8	7	5	4

Desserts

Chocolate Angel Cake
96/serving
pictured on pages 76 and 77

- 1 cup sifted cake flour
- ¾ cup sifted powdered sugar
- 3 tablespoons unsweetened cocoa powder
- 10 egg whites
- 1½ teaspoons cream of tartar
- 1½ teaspoons vanilla
- ¼ teaspoon salt
- 1 cup sifted powdered sugar
  Rum Royale Glaze

Sift together flour, ¾ cup powdered sugar, and cocoa powder into bowl; repeat sifting. Set aside.

In a large mixer bowl beat egg whites with cream of tartar, vanilla, and salt at medium speed of electric mixer till soft peaks form (tips curl over). Gradually add the 1 cup powdered sugar, 2 tablespoons at a time, beating at high speed till stiff peaks form (tips stand straight).

Sift about ¼ cup of the flour mixture over whites; fold in. Repeat, folding in remaining flour by fourths. Turn into an ungreased 9-inch tube pan. Bake on lower rack in a 375° oven for 30 to 35 minutes or till cake tests done.

Invert cake in pan; cool. Using a spatula, loosen cake from pan; remove. Drizzle Rum Royale Glaze over cake. Slice into thin wedges to serve. Makes 16 servings.

Rum Royale Glaze: In small bowl stir together ½ cup *sifted powdered sugar*, ¼ teaspoon *rum extract*, and enough *milk* (about 2 teaspoons) to make of drizzling consistency.

Strawberry Sponge Cake
120/serving

- 1 cup sifted cake flour
- 1¼ cups sifted powdered sugar
- 5 egg yolks
- 5 egg whites
- 1 teaspoon vanilla
- ½ teaspoon cream of tartar
- ½ teaspoon almond extract
- 1 1½-ounce envelope dessert topping mix
- ½ cup skim milk
- ¼ cup currant jelly
- 4 cups fresh whole strawberries, sliced

Combine flour and ½ *cup* of the powdered sugar; set aside. Beat egg yolks on high speed of electric mixer till thick and lemon-colored. Gradually add ½ *cup* of the remaining powdered sugar and ½ teaspoon *salt*, beating constantly. Wash beaters thoroughly. Beat egg whites with vanilla, cream of tartar, and extract till soft peaks form. Gradually add remaining ¼ cup powdered sugar, beating till stiff peaks form. Gently fold yolk mixture into whites. Sift flour mixture over batter, ⅓ at a time; gently fold in just till blended. Turn into an ungreased 10-inch tube pan. Bake in 325° oven for 30 minutes or till cake tests done. Invert cake in pan; cool completely. Remove cake from pan. At serving time, slice cake in half horizontally. Combine dessert topping mix and the skim milk; beat with electric mixer till soft peaks form. In a small saucepan heat jelly till melted. To assemble cake, place one half of cake on a serving plate; spoon *half* of the whipped dessert topping over top of cake. Arrange *half* the berries atop; drizzle with *half* the jelly. Top with remaining cake layer. Spoon remaining whipped topping over cake. Top with remaining berries and melted jelly. Makes 16 servings.

Ambrosia Cream Puffs
131/serving
pictured on pages 76 and 77

- ½ cup orange juice
- 3 tablespoons sugar
- 1 tablespoon cornstarch
- 1 teaspoon finely shredded orange peel
- 1 cup plain yogurt
- 1 medium banana, finely chopped
- 1 egg white
  Cream Puffs (see recipe, below)

In saucepan combine orange juice, *1 tablespoon* of the sugar, cornstarch, and orange peel. Cook and stir till bubbly. Remove from heat; cool slightly. Fold in yogurt and banana. Chill 2 hours. Beat egg white on high speed of electric mixer to soft peaks; gradually add remaining sugar, beating to stiff peaks. Fold into yogurt mixture. Chill. To serve, split and fill Cream Puffs. Serves 8.

Cream Puffs—74/serving

- 2 tablespoons butter *or* margarine
- ½ cup all-purpose flour
- 2 eggs

In saucepan melt butter in ½ cup boiling *water*. Add flour and ⅛ teaspoon *salt* all at once; stir vigorously. Cook and stir till mixture forms a ball that doesn't separate. Remove from heat; cool 10 minutes. Add eggs, one at a time, beating about 30 seconds after each addition. Drop by heaping tablespoonfuls, 3 inches apart, on lightly greased baking sheet. Bake in a 400° oven about 30 minutes or till golden brown and puffy. Remove from oven, cut off tops. Remove soft center. Cool on rack. Makes 8.

Wine Fruit Medley
72/serving

- ⅓ cup orange juice
- ¼ cup port wine
- 1 tablespoon sugar
- 1 tablespoon lemon juice
- 1 cup fresh whole strawberries, sliced
- 1 medium peach, peeled, pitted, and sliced
- 1 medium pear, peeled, cored, and diced
- 1 medium banana, sliced

Combine orange juice, port wine, sugar, and lemon juice. Place cut-up fruits in a bowl. Pour juice mixture over; toss lightly to mix. Cover and chill thoroughly. Makes 6 servings.

Polynesian Parfaits
100/serving

- ½ cup plain yogurt
- 2 teaspoons sugar
- 1 medium banana, sliced
  Lemon juice
- 1 11-ounce can mandarin orange sections, drained
- 1 8-ounce can pineapple chunks (juice pack), drained
  Ground nutmeg

Combine yogurt and sugar. Dip banana slices into lemon juice to prevent darkening. Layer yogurt mixture with banana slices, orange sections, and pineapple chunks in 4 sherbet dishes. Sprinkle each serving with nutmeg. Cover and chill at least 1 hour. Makes 4 servings.

Orange Cake Roll or *Berry-Rice Pudding* (see recipe, page 83) won't ruin your diet!

Orange Cake Roll
135/serving

- 4 egg yolks
- 1 tablespoon frozen orange juice concentrate, thawed
- ½ teaspoon finely shredded orange peel
- ¼ cup granulated sugar
- 4 egg whites
- ⅓ cup granulated sugar
- ½ cup all-purpose flour
- 1 teaspoon baking powder
- ¼ teaspoon salt
  Sifted powdered sugar
- 1 1½-ounce envelope dessert topping mix
- 1 medium orange, peeled, sectioned, and cut up
  Orange slices (optional)
  Finely shredded orange peel (optional)

In small mixer bowl beat yolks at high speed of electric mixer till thick and lemon-colored. Add orange juice concentrate and ½ teaspoon orange peel; beat at low speed till blended. Beat at medium speed till thick. Gradually add the ¼ cup granulated sugar, beating till sugar is dissolved. Wash beaters thoroughly. In large mixer bowl beat egg whites at medium speed of electric mixer till soft peaks form. Gradually add the ⅓ cup granulated sugar; continue beating till stiff peaks form. Fold yolks into whites. Thoroughly stir together flour, baking powder, and salt; sprinkle over egg mixture. Gently fold in flour mixture just till blended. Spread batter evenly in a greased and floured 15x10x1-inch jelly roll pan. Bake in 375° oven for 12 to 15 minutes or till done. Immediately loosen edges of cake from pan and turn out onto towel sprinkled with sifted powdered sugar. Starting with the narrow end, roll the warm cake and towel together; cool on wire rack. Prepare topping mix according to package directions, using skim milk. Fold in cut-up orange. Unroll cake; spread topping mixture over cake, leaving a 1-inch rim. Roll up cake. If desired, garnish with orange slices and orange peel. Serves 10.

Lemon Pudding Cake
109/serving

- 3 egg whites
- ¼ cup sugar
- 3 egg yolks
- 1 teaspoon finely shredded lemon peel
- ¼ cup lemon juice
- 2 tablespoons butter *or* margarine, melted
- ¼ cup sifted all-purpose flour
- 2 tablespoons sugar
- 1½ cups *reconstituted* nonfat dry milk

In a large bowl beat egg whites with dash *salt* on high speed of electric mixer till soft peaks form (tips curl over). Gradually add the ¼ cup sugar, beating to stiff peaks (tips stand straight). In another bowl beat egg yolks with lemon peel, lemon juice, and butter or margarine. Combine flour and 2 tablespoons sugar; stir along with milk into egg yolk mixture. Fold in egg whites. Pour batter into an ungreased 8x8x2-inch baking pan. Place in larger pan on oven rack. Pour hot water to a depth of 1 inch into larger pan. Bake in 350° oven for 35 to 40 minutes. Serve warm or chilled. Makes 9 servings.

Coffee Meringues
107/serving

Individual Meringue Shells
3 beaten egg yolks
¼ cup sugar
¼ cup *reconstituted* nonfat dry milk
2 teaspoons instant coffee crystals
Dash salt
1 1½-ounce envelope dessert topping mix
1 stiff-beaten egg white

Prepare Individual Meringue Shells. Cool thoroughly.

In small saucepan combine egg yolks, sugar, ¼ cup milk, coffee crystals, and salt. Cook over low heat, stirring constantly, till mixture coats a metal spoon. Remove from heat. Cool quickly by placing pan in a bowl of ice water; stir till mixture is cooled.

Prepare topping mix according to package directions *except* use skim milk or reconstituted nonfat dry milk. Fold topping and egg white into cooled cooked mixture. Chill. To serve, spoon into meringue shells. Makes 10 servings.

Individual Meringue Shells: Let 2 *egg whites* come to room temperature. Add ½ teaspoon *vanilla*, ¼ teaspoon *cream of tartar*, and dash *salt*. Beat till soft peaks form (tips curl over). Gradually add ½ cup *sugar*, beating till stiff peaks form (tips stand straight) and sugar is dissolved. Line baking sheet with plain brown paper. Draw ten 2½-inch circles on paper; spread each with some of the meringue. Using back of spoon, shape into shells. Bake in 300° oven about 35 minutes. (For crisper meringues, turn off oven. Dry meringues in oven with door closed about 1 hour more.) Makes 10.

Choco-Mint Roll—125/serving

4 egg yolks
Few drops red food coloring
¼ cup granulated sugar
4 egg whites
¼ cup granulated sugar
½ cup sifted cake flour
¼ cup unsweetened cocoa powder
1 teaspoon baking powder
1 tablespoon powdered sugar
⅓ cup granulated sugar
⅓ cup nonfat dry milk powder
2 tablespoons cornstarch
2 well-beaten eggs
Few drops peppermint extract

In small mixer bowl beat 4 yolks about 5 minutes or till thick and lemon-colored. Add food coloring. Gradually add ¼ cup granulated sugar, beating till sugar dissolves. Wash beaters thoroughly. In large mixer bowl beat 4 egg whites to soft peaks; gradually add ¼ cup granulated sugar, beating to stiff peaks. Fold yolks into whites. Sift together flour, cocoa, baking powder, and ¼ teaspoon *salt*; fold into egg mixture. Spread evenly in a greased and waxed paper-lined 15x10x1-inch jelly roll pan. Bake in 375° oven for 10 to 12 minutes. Loosen sides; turn out onto a towel sprinkled with the powdered sugar. Carefully peel off paper. Starting at narrow end, roll cake and towel together; cool thoroughly on wire rack.

To prepare filling, in saucepan combine ⅓ cup granulated sugar, the milk powder, cornstarch, and dash *salt*. Add 1 cup *water*. Cook and stir over medium heat till bubbly; cook and stir 2 minutes more. Remove from heat. Stir about half of the hot mixture into the 2 beaten eggs; return all to saucepan. Cook and stir just till bubbly; cook and stir 2 minutes more. Remove from heat; add extract. Cover with clear plastic wrap; cool. Unroll cake; spread with filling. Roll up. Cover; chill. Serves 12.

Stirred Custard—112/serving

3 beaten eggs
3 tablespoons sugar
Dash salt
2 cups *reconstituted* nonfat dry milk
½ teaspoon vanilla
Ground nutmeg

In top of double boiler combine eggs, sugar, salt, and milk. Cook and stir over hot (not boiling) water till mixture coats a metal spoon. Remove from heat and cool slightly. Stir in vanilla. Cool completely. Turn into dessert dishes. Cover and chill. To serve, sprinkle with nutmeg. Makes 5 servings.

Note: If desired, serve Stirred Custard over fresh fruit.

Citrus-Cheese Sauce
16/tablespoon

4 ounces Neufchâtel cheese, softened
3 tablespoons sugar
1 teaspoon finely shredded orange peel
½ teaspoon finely shredded lemon peel
1 tablespoon orange juice
1 tablespoon lemon juice
⅓ cup nonfat dry milk powder
⅓ cup ice water

In a small bowl beat together cheese, sugar, orange peel, lemon peel, orange juice, and lemon juice on low speed of electric mixer till smooth. Cover and chill. To serve, in mixing bowl combine milk powder and ice water; beat till stiff peaks form (tips stand straight). Fold into cheese mixture (do not overmix). Serve over cake or fruit. Makes about 2 cups.

Berry-Rice Pudding 108/serving

This updated old favorite, but with fewer calories, is pictured on page 80—

1⅓ cups water
⅔ cup evaporated skimmed milk
⅓ cup long grain rice
1 beaten egg yolk
2 tablespoons sugar
2 tablespoons lemon juice
¼ teaspoon salt
1 teaspoon vanilla
¼ teaspoon grated lemon peel
3 egg whites
¼ teaspoon cream of tartar
2 tablespoons sugar
1 cup sliced fresh
      strawberries
   Finely shredded lemon peel
8 whole fresh strawberries

In medium saucepan combine water, evaporated skimmed milk, and rice. Bring to boiling. Reduce heat; cook, covered, over low heat for 20 minutes, stirring often. Uncover; cook 5 minutes more. In a small bowl combine egg yolk, 2 tablespoons sugar, lemon juice, and salt. Stir about *1 cup* of the hot mixture into yolk mixture; return all to saucepan. Bring to a gentle boil. Cook and stir over low heat for 3 to 4 minutes or till slightly thickened. Remove from heat; stir in vanilla and lemon peel. Cool mixture thoroughly.

In a medium bowl beat egg whites and cream of tartar on high speed of electric mixer till soft peaks form (tips curl over). Gradually add 2 tablespoons sugar, beating till stiff peaks form (tips stand straight). Fold egg whites into cooled pudding. Fold in sliced berries; spoon mixture into 8 sherbet dishes. Cover and chill several hours. To serve, garnish with finely shredded lemon peel and whole strawberries. Makes 8 servings.

Dessert Topping Tips

The kind of whipped topping you use on your diet dessert can make a big difference in your dessert's total calorie count. For example, regular whipping cream, whipped and sweetened, has 28 calories per tablespoon; frozen whipped dessert topping adds 14 calories per tablespoon; the same amount of topping from a mix (made with whole milk) totals just 10 calories.

Steamed Cranberry Pudding 137/serving

1 cup all-purpose flour
1 teaspoon baking soda
¼ teaspoon ground cinnamon
¼ teaspoon ground nutmeg
   Dash ground cloves
⅓ cup hot water
⅓ cup light molasses
¼ cup packed brown sugar
1 cup halved fresh *or*
      frozen cranberries
½ of a 4½-ounce container
      frozen whipped
      dessert topping, thawed

In a medium mixing bowl stir together all-purpose flour, baking soda, cinnamon, nutmeg, and cloves. In a small mixing bowl combine hot water, light molasses, and brown sugar; stir into flour mixture along with halved cranberries. Pour batter into a greased 1-quart mold. Cover with greased foil; tie securely with string.

Place mold on rack in deep kettle; add boiling water to a depth of 1 inch to kettle. Cover; steam for 2½ hours, adding more boiling water to kettle, if necessary. Cool steamed pudding 10 minutes; unmold. Serve warm with whipped topping. Makes 8 servings.

Lemon Soufflé—102/serving

Make this delicately flavored light dessert for your next dinner party. It's easy to make a day ahead—

1 envelope unflavored gelatin
¼ cup lemon juice
¼ cup water
2 egg yolks
2 tablespoons sugar
1 cup skim milk
2 egg whites
1 1½-ounce envelope dessert
      topping mix
   Shredded lemon peel
   (optional)
   Lemon slices (optional)

In small saucepan soften unflavored gelatin in lemon juice and water; heat just till gelatin is dissolved. Remove from heat.

In small mixer bowl beat egg yolks on high speed of electric mixer; gradually add sugar, beating about 5 minutes or till thick and lemon-colored. Gradually beat in hot gelatin mixture; beat in milk. Cool till mixture is partially set (consistency of unbeaten egg whites). Wash beaters thoroughly. Beat egg whites just till stiff peaks form (tips stand straight); *do not overbeat*. Fold in gelatin mixture. Prepare dessert topping mix according to package directions, *except* use skim milk. Fold ¼ cup of the prepared topping into gelatin mixture (refrigerate remaining topping for another use). Pour gelatin mixture into a 3-cup soufflé dish with foil collar. (*Or*, use a 4-cup soufflé dish without collar or use six ½-cup individual soufflé dishes.) Refrigerate at least 3 hours or till set. To serve, remove foil collar. Garnish with shredded lemon peel and slices, if desired. Makes 6 servings.

Note: If desired, use the remaining whipped dessert topping to garnish each serving. One tablespoon whipped dessert topping made with whole milk adds 10 calories to the calorie count per serving.

Yogurt-Sauced Peaches
87/serving

You can substitute your favorite in-season fruits for the peaches—

- ½ cup cream-style cottage cheese
- ⅓ cup skim milk
- 2 tablespoons sugar
- 1 teaspoon lemon juice
- ⅛ teaspoon ground cardamom
  Few drops almond extract
- ½ cup plain yogurt
- 8 fresh medium peaches *or* two 16-ounce cans peach slices (juice pack)

In blender container or food processor bowl combine cottage cheese, skim milk, sugar, lemon juice, cardamom, and almond extract. Cover; process till smooth. Fold in yogurt. Chill. At serving time, peel, pit, and slice fresh peaches (*or*, drain canned peaches). Divide peach slices between 8 sherbet dishes. Spoon sauce over peaches. Serves 8.

Chocolate Bavarian
87/serving

- ⅔ cup nonfat dry milk powder
- ⅓ cup sugar
- 2 tablespoons cornstarch
- 2 tablespoons unsweetened cocoa powder
- 1 envelope unflavored gelatin
- ⅛ teaspoon salt
- 1½ cups cold water
- 3 beaten egg yolks
- 2 egg whites
- 1 teaspoon vanilla
- ¼ teaspoon cream of tartar
- ½ of a 4½-ounce container frozen whipped dessert topping, thawed

In saucepan combine the dry milk powder, sugar, cornstarch, cocoa powder, gelatin, and salt. Stir in cold water. Cook and stir over medium heat till thickened and bubbly. Stir about *half* of the hot mixture into egg yolks; return all to saucepan. Bring to a gentle boil. Cook and stir 1 minute more. Cool. In a medium mixer bowl beat egg whites, vanilla, and cream of tartar on high speed of electric mixer till stiff peaks form (tips stand straight). Fold into cooled chocolate mixture. Fold in whipped dessert topping. Turn into a 4- or 5-cup mold. Chill several hours or overnight or till firm. Garnish with additional whipped topping, if desired. Serves 10.

Rum Custard Soufflé
88/serving

- ½ cup nonfat dry milk powder
- ⅓ cup sugar
- 1 envelope unflavored gelatin
- ¼ teaspoon salt
- 1½ cups cold water
- 4 beaten egg yolks
- ½ teaspoon rum flavoring
- 4 egg whites
  Ground nutmeg

In saucepan combine milk powder, sugar, gelatin, and salt; stir in cold water. Stir in egg yolks. Cook and stir over medium heat till mixture just coats a metal spoon. Remove from heat; stir in rum flavoring. Chill till partially set (consistency of unbeaten egg whites); stir occasionally. In a large mixer bowl beat egg whites on high speed of electric mixer to stiff peaks (tips stand straight); fold into gelatin mixture. Turn into a 4-cup soufflé dish with foil collar; sprinkle with nutmeg. Chill several hours or overnight or till firm. Serves 8.

Fresh Fruit Substitutes

If your favorite fruits are not in season, you can purchase them canned or frozen for little difference in calories. For canned fruits, choose juice pack, water pack, or calorie-reduced pack (slightly sweetened). If you use regular syrup-pack fruits, rinse the fruit with water before using. In frozen fruit, look for the unsweetened loose pack variety.

Apricot Spanish Cream
105/serving

This rich-tasting delight is pictured on pages 76 and 77—

- 1 16-ounce can unpeeled apricot halves
- 1 envelope unflavored gelatin
- ¼ cup sugar
  Dash salt
- 1 cup *reconstituted* nonfat dry milk
- 2 beaten egg yolks
- 2 egg whites
  Mint sprigs

Drain apricot halves, reserving ¾ cup liquid; halve apricot halves and set aside. In saucepan combine gelatin, sugar, and salt; stir in reserved apricot liquid, milk, and beaten egg yolks. Cook and stir over low heat till gelatin and sugar dissolve. Remove from heat; chill till partially set (consistency of unbeaten egg whites). Beat egg whites on high speed of electric mixer till stiff peaks form (tips stand straight). Fold into gelatin mixture. Turn into six individual molds. Chill till firm. Unmold. Garnish with reserved apricots and mint sprigs. Makes 6 servings.

Lime Freeze—74/serving

For Lemon Freeze, simply substitute lemon peel and juice for the lime peel and juice, and add yellow food coloring, if desired. Both variations are pictured on pages 76 and 77—

- ½ cup evaporated skimmed milk
- 2 egg yolks
- ⅓ cup sugar
- ½ teaspoon grated lime peel
- 2 tablespoons lime juice
  Dash salt
- 3 or 4 drops green food coloring (optional)
- 2 egg whites
- 2 tablespoons lime juice
  Lime or lemon twists

Pour milk into shallow container; freeze till icy cold. In a mixing bowl combine egg yolks, sugar, lime peel, 2 tablespoons lime juice, salt, and food coloring; set aside. In another bowl beat the icy milk and egg whites with electric mixer till fluffy. Add 2 tablespoons lime juice; beat till stiff peaks form (tips stand straight). Beat in egg yolk mixture. Pour into 8x4x2-inch loaf pan; freeze firm. With a fork, break mixture into chunks. In chilled mixer bowl beat with electric mixer for 5 to 6 minutes or till smooth. Return to loaf pan; freeze firm. Scoop to serve; garnish with lime or lemon twists. Makes 8 servings.

Pineapple Fluff 97/serving

- 1 8-ounce can crushed pineapple (juice pack)
- 3 tablespoons nonfat dry milk powder
- 2 beaten egg yolks
- 1 tablespoon sugar
- ½ teaspoon vanilla
- 2 egg whites
- 1 tablespoon sugar

Drain pineapple well, reserving juice. Chill pineapple. Add water to reserved juice, if necessary, to make ½ cup. Dissolve dry milk powder in pineapple juice. In a small heavy saucepan combine the milk mixture, egg yolks, and 1 tablespoon sugar; cook over low heat, stirring constantly till mixture thickens and coats a metal spoon. Remove from heat; place saucepan in a pan of ice water to cool. Stir in vanilla. When cooled, cover and chill 2 to 4 hours.

At serving time, fold pineapple into cooked mixture. In a small mixer bowl beat egg whites on high speed of electric mixer till soft peaks form (tips curl over); gradually add 1 tablespoon sugar, beating till stiff peaks form (tips stand straight). Gently fold egg whites into the pineapple mixture. Spoon into chilled serving dishes. Serve immediately. Makes 4 servings.

Peach Dessert Sauce 47/serving

Try this dessert sauce over fresh raspberries, too—

- 1½ cups chopped fresh or frozen unsweetened peaches
- ¼ cup sugar
- 2 teaspoons cornstarch
- ½ teaspoon finely shredded lemon peel
- ¼ teaspoon ground cinnamon
- ¼ teaspoon ground nutmeg
  Dash salt
- ⅓ cup water
- 8 scoops (⅓ cup each) lemon or vanilla frozen yogurt

Mash ¾ cup of the chopped peaches; set aside. In saucepan stir together sugar, cornstarch, lemon peel, cinnamon, nutmeg, and salt. Add water; mix well. Stir in mashed peaches and chopped peaches. Cook and stir till thickened and bubbly. Reduce heat; simmer for 5 to 7 minutes or till desired consistency, stirring occasionally. Remove from heat; serve warm over scoops of lemon or vanilla frozen yogurt. Makes 8 servings.

Maple Dessert Cups 66/serving

- 1 envelope unflavored gelatin
- 2 tablespoons brown sugar
- ⅔ cup evaporated skimmed milk
- ½ teaspoon maple flavoring
- 1 egg white
- 1 tablespoon brown sugar
- ½ of a 4½-ounce container frozen dessert topping, thawed

In saucepan combine gelatin and 2 tablespoons brown sugar; stir in ½ cup cold water. Cook and stir over medium heat till gelatin and sugar dissolve. Remove from heat; stir in evaporated skimmed milk and maple flavoring. Pour mixture into large bowl; chill till almost set.

Beat egg white and 1 tablespoon brown sugar till stiff peaks form (tips stand straight). Beat chilled gelatin mixture using electric mixer till light and fluffy. Fold in beaten egg white. Spoon into 8 sherbet dishes. Chill till firm. To serve, top each serving with a spoonful of dessert topping. Makes 8 servings.

Calorie-Trimmed
Beverages & Snacks

Low-calorie foods for between-meal snacking include
(from left) *Strawberry-Yogurt Drink, Cottage
Cheese–Tomato Appetizers, Potted Pepper Dip,* and
Raspberry Sparkle Punch. (See index for recipe pages.)

Calorie-Trimmed
Beverages & Snacks

Snacks probably are the biggest offenders when it comes to upsetting the nutrition in a good diet. Too often they consist only of "empty" calories—calories accompanied by little, if any, nutritional value. Snacks also can sap your mealtime appetite, causing you to bypass more nutritious foods throughout the day. Good snacks should be just enough to tide you to your next meal and be as nutritious and as appetizing as possible.

The best snacks are small amounts of any meat, grain, fruit, vegetable, or milk-based food group. Limit them to two or three pieces. Keep protein snacks one-fourth to one-third the size of a main dish portion. To carry you over from one meal to another try a hard-cooked egg, some fruit, a cold soup, or vegetable nibblers. Don't forget about beverages for fast and easy perk-ups. Use your blender to whip up a frothy fruit drink.

NUTRITIONAL ANALYSIS

| | Per Serving | | | | | | Percent U.S. RDA Per Serving | | | | | | | |
	CALORIES	PROTEIN gms.	CARBOHYDRATE gms.	FAT gms.	SODIUM mgs.	POTASSIUM mgs.	PROTEIN	VITAMIN A	VITAMIN C	THIAMINE	RIBOFLAVIN	NIACIN	CALCIUM	IRON
Blue Cheese Dip (p. 92)	13	2	1	0	42	15	3	1	1	0	2	0	2	0
Cottage Cheese-Tomato Appetizers (p. 90)	9	1	2	0	28	85	1	6	13	1	1	1	1	1
Cranberry Fruit Dip (p. 90)	24	1	5	0	7	27	1	0	2	0	1	0	2	0
Curried-Stuffed Eggs (p. 90)	25	2	0	2	43	21	3	4	1	1	2	0	1	2
Eggnog (p. 89)	61	4	7	2	91	120	7	3	1	2	10	11	9	1
Frothy Apple Cooler (p. 89)	59	2	13	0	23	167	2	0	2	2	6	1	6	3
Oatmeal Cookies (p. 92)	30	1	4	1	40	14	1	1	0	1	1	0	0	1
Orange-Peach Refresher (p. 89)	69	2	15	0	24	332	4	20	60	6	8	5	7	3
Potted Pepper Dip (p. 92)	15	1	1	1	73	30	1	1	18	1	1	1	1	0
Raspberry Sparkle Punch (p. 89)	32	0	0	0	0	26	0	0	11	0	1	1	0	1
Spiced Hot Cocoa (p. 89)	92	7	16	1	99	379	11	0	2	5	21	1	25	3
Spinach Dip (p. 90)	39	1	1	4	69	47	1	10	9	1	2	0	2	1
Strawberry-Yogurt Drink (p. 89)	93	5	17	1	109	353	7	3	44	5	15	3	15	3
Vegetable Cheese Dip (p. 90)	22	1	1	2	37	36	1	10	9	0	1	0	1	0
Vegetable Refresher (p. 89)	31	2	6	0	216	267	4	11	16	4	6	4	6	3
Whole Wheat Biscuit Crackers (p. 92)	40	1	5	2	87	17	1	2	0	2	1	1	1	1

Beverages

Strawberry-Yogurt Drink
93/serving
pictured on pages 86 and 87

- 1 cup fresh *or* frozen unsweetened whole strawberries
- 1 cup buttermilk
- 1 8-ounce carton plain yogurt
- 1 ripe large banana, cut up
- 8 ice cubes

Thaw strawberries, if frozen. In blender container combine buttermilk, yogurt, banana, ice cubes, and strawberries. Cover and blend till smooth. Makes 4 servings.

Orange-Peach Refresher
69/serving

- 2 medium peaches *or* 4 medium apricots
- 1 cup orange juice
- ¼ cup nonfat dry milk powder
- 8 ice cubes

Peel and pit peaches or apricots. In blender container combine orange juice, milk powder, ice cubes, and fruit. Cover and blend till smooth. Pour into 2 glasses. Garnish with additional peach or apricot slices and mint sprigs, if desired. Serves 2.

Frothy Apple Cooler
59/serving

- 1½ cups apple juice, chilled
- ¼ cup nonfat dry milk powder
- ¼ teaspoon ground cinnamon
- 3 ice cubes

In blender container combine apple juice, milk powder, cinnamon, and ice cubes. Cover and blend till smooth. Serve immediately. Makes 4 servings.

Raspberry Sparkle Punch
32/serving
pictured on pages 86 and 87

- 1 10-ounce package frozen red raspberries, thawed
- 1 6-ounce can (¾ cup) frozen lemonade concentrate, thawed
  Fruited Ice Ring
- 2 16-ounce bottles low-calorie lemon-lime carbonated beverage

Sieve raspberries; discard seeds. Combine sieved berries, lemonade concentrate, and 2 cups *water*. Chill. At serving time pour the raspberry mixture into punch bowl. Add Fruited Ice Ring; carefully pour in the carbonated beverage. Makes 16 four-ounce servings.

Fruited Ice Ring: Arrange orange slices, lemon slices, and mint sprigs in bottom of ring mold. Fill with cold water. Freeze till firm. Unmold before placing in punch bowl.

Eggnog—61/serving

- 4 egg yolks
- ¼ cup sugar
- 4 cups *reconstituted* nonfat dry milk
- 1 teaspoon vanilla
- ¼ teaspoon brandy flavoring
- 4 egg whites
  Ground nutmeg

Beat egg yolks, sugar, and ¼ teaspoon *salt*; stir in *2 cups* of the milk. Cook and stir over medium heat till mixture coats a metal spoon. Remove from heat; add remaining milk. Stir in vanilla and brandy flavoring. Cover and chill.

To serve, beat egg whites till soft peaks form. Carefully fold yolk mixture into beaten egg whites. Serve eggnog in cups; sprinkle with nutmeg. Makes 14 four-ounce servings.

Vegetable Refresher
31/serving

- ½ medium cucumber
- 2 cups vegetable juice cocktail, chilled
- 1 cup buttermilk

Peel cucumber; halve lengthwise and remove seeds. Cut cucumber into pieces. In blender container combine chilled vegetable juice cocktail, buttermilk, and cucumber. Cover and blend till cucumber is puréed. Serve cold. Makes 6 servings.

Spiced Hot Cocoa
92/serving

- ¼ cup unsweetened cocoa powder
- 2 tablespoons sugar
  Dash salt
- 1 cup water
- 6 inches stick cinnamon
- 6 whole cloves
- 1⅓ cups nonfat dry milk powder
- 3 cups water
- ¼ teaspoon vanilla
- ⅓ cup nonfat dry milk powder
- ⅓ cup ice water

In saucepan combine unsweetened cocoa powder, sugar, and salt; add the 1 cup water, stick cinnamon, and cloves. Bring to boiling, stirring constantly. Reduce heat; simmer for 5 minutes.

Reconstitute the 1⅓ cups nonfat dry milk powder in the 3 cups water. Add to chocolate mixture. Bring just to boiling; stir in vanilla. Remove cinnamon sticks and cloves.

In mixer bowl combine ⅓ cup nonfat dry milk powder and ⅓ cup ice water; beat at high speed of electric mixer till stiff peaks form.

Pour hot cocoa into 6 heatproof mugs; top with whipped milk. Serve with more stick cinnamon stirrers, if desired. Makes 6 servings.

Snacks

Cottage Cheese-Tomato Appetizers—9/appetizer

pictured on pages 86 and 87

- 24 cherry tomatoes
- ¼ cup dry cottage cheese
- ½ medium cucumber, shredded and drained
- ¼ teaspoon salt
  Dash dried dillweed
  Dash pepper

Cut small slice off bottoms of cherry tomatoes so they will sit flat. Cut thin slice from tops of tomatoes. With small melon baller or spoon carefully scoop out centers of tomatoes; discard. Sprinkle insides with a little salt and pepper. Invert and chill.

In bowl combine cottage cheese, shredded cucumber, salt, dillweed, and pepper. Cover and chill.

To serve, spoon a small amount of cottage cheese mixture into each cherry tomato. Makes 24.

Curried-Stuffed Eggs 25/appetizer

- 5 hard-cooked eggs
- 3 tablespoons dairy sour cream
- 1 tablespoon snipped parsley
- 2 teaspoons skim milk
- ½ teaspoon curry powder
- ¼ teaspoon salt

Quarter hard-cooked eggs lengthwise. Remove yolks to bowl; mash. Combine yolks, sour cream, parsley, skim milk, curry, and salt. If necessary, cut a thin slice off the bottom of each egg quarter so it will sit flat. Using pastry bag with star tip, pipe sour cream mixture into egg whites. Chill. Makes 20.

Vegetable Dippers

Enjoy tasty dips and cut calories at the same time by serving raw vegetables for dipping. Crisp, cold carrots, celery, green pepper, cucumber, zucchini, broccoli, cherry tomatoes, cauliflower flowerets, mushrooms, and radishes are colorful and fresh tasting. Peel the vegetables if necessary, then serve whole or cut into appropriate shapes and sizes.

Spinach Dip—39/tablespoon

- 1 cup finely torn and lightly packed fresh spinach leaves
- ½ cup lightly packed parsley (stems removed)
- ¼ cup water
- 3 tablespoons chopped green onion
- ¼ teaspoon dried tarragon, crushed
- ⅔ cup plain yogurt
- ⅓ cup mayonnaise or salad dressing
- ¼ teaspoon salt
  Assorted vegetables for dipping

In small saucepan combine torn spinach leaves, parsley, water, green onion, and tarragon. Bring to boiling. Reduce heat; cover and simmer for 1 minute. Drain vegetables, discarding liquid.

Purée vegetables; stir in yogurt, mayonnaise or salad dressing, and salt. Cover and chill. Serve with vegetable dippers. Makes 1 cup.

Cranberry Fruit Dip 24/tablespoon

- 1 8-ounce carton vanilla yogurt
- ½ cup cranberry-orange relish
- ¼ teaspoon ground nutmeg
- ¼ teaspoon ground ginger
  Assorted fruits for dipping (strawberries, apple slices, mandarin orange sections, and pineapple slices)

In a small bowl combine vanilla yogurt, cranberry-orange relish, nutmeg, and ginger; mix till well blended. Cover and chill. Serve with assorted fruits for dipping. If desired, garnish with a strawberry and several mint sprigs. Makes about 1¼ cups dip.

Vegetable Cheese Dip 22/tablespoon

- ½ of an 8-ounce package Neufchâtel cheese
- ½ cup chopped carrot
- ¼ cup chopped green pepper
- ¼ cup chopped celery
- 2 tablespoons chopped pimiento
- 2 teaspoons lemon juice
- 1 teaspoon Worcestershire sauce
- ⅛ teaspoon pepper
  Assorted vegetables for dipping

In blender container or food processor bowl combine Neufchâtel cheese, carrot, green pepper, celery, pimiento, lemon juice, Worcestershire sauce, and pepper; cover and blend till smooth. (Mixture may have curdled appearance.) Cover and chill. Serve with vegetable dippers. Makes about 1 cup.

Select several fruit dippers to scoop up spicy, yogurt-flavored *Cranberry Fruit Dip.*

Snacks

Potted Pepper Dip
15/tablespoon
pictured on pages 86 and 87

    4 large sweet red *or* green
       peppers
    1 small onion, cut up
    1 tablespoon lemon juice
    2 teaspoons cooking oil
    1 teaspoon salt
    ½ teaspoon prepared
       horseradish
       Dash pepper
    ¾ cup plain yogurt
    ½ of an 8-ounce package
       Neufchâtel cheese, softened
       Few dashes bottled hot
       pepper sauce
       Assorted vegetables for
       dipping

Quarter peppers lengthwise; remove stem and seeds. Place peppers, peel side up, on baking sheet. Broil 2 to 3 inches from heat for 4 to 5 minutes or till peppers are charred. Cool, then peel peppers.

In blender container or food processor bowl place about ⅓ of the red or green peppers, the onion, lemon juice, cooking oil, salt, horseradish, and pepper. Cover and blend till smooth. Add another ⅓ of the peppers to mixture in blender container or food processor bowl; cover and blend till smooth. Repeat with remaining peppers. Transfer mixture to bowl. Cover and let stand at room temperature for 2 hours.

Sieve vegetable mixture, pressing gently to drain off excess liquid. In mixing bowl combine yogurt, Neufchâtel cheese, and hot pepper sauce. Stir in sieved vegetable mixture. Cover; chill. If desired, spoon into 2 hollow green pepper shells; keep 1 shell chilled while serving the other. Serve with vegetable dippers. Makes 2⅓ cups.

Sensible Snacking

When watching your weight, remember to count calories from snacks. Here are some helpful calorie-cutting snack ideas:
• Reserve a part of a meal, such as the salad or dessert, for an afternoon or late-evening snack.
• Snack on foods that provide part of your nutritional needs, not "empty" calories. For example, a milk-based beverage supplies calcium, protein, and vitamins A and D, and a meat sandwich provides protein.
• Eat fresh fruits and vegetables, which are low in calories, for excellent snacks.
• Make sandwiches with thin-sliced bread. Or, serve open-face sandwiches.
• Cut calories by flavoring yogurt yourself. Just add crushed fruit and a little sugar to plain yogurt.

Blue Cheese Dip
13/tablespoon

    1 cup dry cottage cheese
    3 tablespoons buttermilk
    2 tablespoons crumbled blue
       cheese
    2 tablespoons chopped green
       onion
    1 tablespoon snipped parsley
    1 teaspoon Worcestershire
       sauce
       Dash bottled hot pepper sauce
       Assorted vegetables for
       dipping

In blender container combine cottage cheese, buttermilk, blue cheese, green onion, parsley, Worcestershire, and hot pepper sauce. Cover; blend till smooth. Cover and chill. Serve with vegetable dippers. Makes 1 cup.

Whole Wheat Biscuit Crackers—40/cracker

    ½ cup whole wheat flour
    ½ cup all-purpose flour
    2 tablespoons sugar
    1 teaspoon baking powder
    ½ teaspoon baking soda
    ¼ teaspoon cream of tartar
    ¼ teaspoon salt
    ¼ cup butter *or* margarine
    ⅓ cup buttermilk

In bowl combine dry ingredients; cut in butter till mixture resembles coarse crumbs. Add buttermilk. Stir with fork just till dough follows fork around bowl. On floured surface roll out to ¼-inch thickness. Using floured 2½-inch biscuit cutter cut dough into 12 circles. Place on ungreased baking sheet. Bake in 350° oven for 12 to 15 minutes or till lightly browned.

Reduce oven temperature to 300°. Split hot biscuits with sharp knife; place cut sides up on baking sheet. Dry in 300° oven for 12 to 15 minutes. Makes 24.

Oatmeal Cookies
30/cookie

    ½ cup all-purpose flour
    ¼ cup granulated sugar
    ½ teaspoon baking soda
    ½ teaspoon baking powder
    ¼ cup packed brown sugar
    ¼ cup butter, softened
    1 egg
    2 tablespoons plain yogurt
    ¼ teaspoon vanilla
    1 cup quick-cooking rolled oats

Mix flour, granulated sugar, soda, baking powder, and ¼ teaspoon *salt*. Add brown sugar, butter, egg, yogurt, and vanilla; beat well. Stir in oats; chill. Drop from teaspoon onto greased cookie sheet. Bake in 375° oven about 8 minutes. Makes 48.

Index

E-K

L-R

Index